JOURNAL OF THE NEPAL RESEARCH CENTRE

VOL. I
(HUMANITIES)

KOMMISSIONSVERLAG FRANZ STEINER GMBH
WIESBADEN/BRD

1977

ISBN 3-515-02631-2

Printed in Nepal

by University Press

Tribhuvan University, Kathmandu.

TABLE OF CONTENTS

Preface

The present journal (*abbr*. JNRC) is the first one to be published by foreign scientists working in or on Nepal whose mother tongue is not the English language. It is intended to communicate quickly the research results of the scholars working at/from the Nepal Research Centre to the Nepalese scholars and to an interested general public.

At the same time, it also aims at re-publishing in the English language some of the more significant articles on Nepal, originally written in the German language which otherwise would escape the attention of Nepalese scholars: German publications often still are unattainable both because of the feeble nature of book supply from overseas as well as of the language barrier.

Thirdly, the journal will also contain the English translation of outstanding articles written in the Nepali language, which because of similar reasons would escape the attention of Western scholars interested in Nepal or in Hindu and Buddhist studies.

This first volume already contains some examples of the three categories just mentioned.

It is hoped that in this way, exchange of research results, communication of ideas, and stimulation of mutual research contacts can be furthered between the Nepalese and foreign scholars.

The first volume of this journal is being released on the opening day of the new building of the Nepal Research Centre and the Goethe-Institute (German Cultural Centre). Centrally located as it is now, we hope the new Centre to become a meeting place for Nepalese and foreign scientists; the Centre's facilities are being made available to all bona fide scholars. We hope that the official inauguration of the new Nepal Research Centre will mark the beginning of a new period of co-operation between the Nepalese and foreign scholars, the Tribhuvan University and the concerned Departments of His Majesty's Government.

The present volume only contains articles from various fields of humanities. The next volume is proposed to cover various branches of natural and applied, development-orientated sciences.

The editor thanks Mr. Jang B. Thapa for typing most of the articles of this volume, Mr. Mahes Raj Pant for editorial assistance, Dr. M. Witzel for editing and lay-out, the Sahayogi Press, Kathmandu, for their speedy composition and printing, and the University Press, Kirtipur, for precise and quick work in final lay-out and off-set printing.

WOLFGANG VOIGT

Ritual as Mediator of Space in Kathmandu

Niels Gutschow and Manabajra Bajracharya

1. Introduction

The town of Kāṭhmāṇḍu is situated in a valley which only during the past two centuries has come to be the heart of the country of Nepal. In former times, this valley formed one of the important stages on the ancient trade route that connected India and Tibet. Its population during the Middle Ages consisted chiefly of Newars, a Mongoloid people of Tibeto-Burman tongue, who of old are wont to settle in compact settlements. This is in marked distinction to other tribes of Nepal who prefer scattered settlements on the slopes of hills.

Like Pāṭan and Bhaktapur, the two other big Newar towns, Kāṭhmāṇḍu originated from a number of separate nuclei which in the course of time grew together. This process seems to have taken place after AD 1000. It was the 17th century, however, which saw the extension that determines the present state of the city of Kāṭhmāṇḍu: a rectangular grid, deviating by some 15 degrees from the cardinal directions, was superimposed onto the old town. The older pattern is preserved to this day, diagonally cutting through the new outlay. There is no doubt the innovations of the 17th century were due to conscious planning according to principles laid down in the *vāstu-śastra*[1].

The population of Kāṭhmāṇḍu was traditionally Buddhist. Hence, the districts the town in divided into (nepl. *ṭol,* new. *tvaḥ*) were organized round the 18 chief Buddhist monasteries (*mahāvihāra*), who alone held the right of initiation.

The account of the *Pīṭhapūjā* is part of a research project on 'concepts of space' in Nepal (Bhaktapur, Kāṭhmāṇḍu, Pāṭan) and India (Varāṇasi, Mathurā, Purī). Repeated field surveys were made possible by grants of the **German Research Society** (DFG) from 1974–1976.

This paper was first presented at the 30. International Congress of Human Sciences in Asia and North Africa, which was held at Mexico City, 3.–8. August 1976.

I am very much indebted to BERNHARD KÖLVER for discussions on the philosophical interpretations of the *pīṭhapūjā* and translation of this paper into English.

1. *Vāstu-Śāstra,* Vol. I : Hindu Science of Architecture (ed. and transl. by D.N. SHUKLA), Lucknow, without date

This movement had considerable social effects and is clearly mirrored in the structure of Newar towns. Kings not only built a great many temples, but they also installed rites to connect them with each other: thus we see various models of sanctification which aimed at integrating city or kingdom, in order to ensure protection by a particular god or group of gods.

This process entailed a fundamental re-structuring of sacred space : shrines which had been founded immemorial times ago as the seats of pre-Hindu, and probably pre-Buddhist, deities were filled with a new content, were given new interpretations, and thus were absorbed into new spatial patterns.

The idea of organizing space, present in traces from the time of the Upanishads onwards, seems to have been reinforced by the early sects of Tantrik Hinduism. It of course goes back to the old idea of the *pradakṣinā,* i. e. to the need to distinguish between uninhabited and therefore dangerous areas and those which were the seat of human habitatins and their gods[2].

It was not long until the Buddhists adopted such models: although they are at times difficult to reconcile with orthodox Buddhist creed, their emotional appeal must have been such that thinkers made an effort to bring them into line with orthodoxy. It is one of these adaptations that I am about to sketch.

Among the people who are organized around a *mahāvihāra,* the most important group are its Bajrācāryas.Now,members of such families used to form groups in order to perform a ritual called *pīṭhapūjā.*This is, in name, a *pūjā* addressed to the *seats* of certain gods – but according to Tantrik views those advanced in religion can by means of thought project a mental image of a deity onto a particular place – and we should remember that among Nepalese Buddhists, the Bajrācāryas are the most advanced group. Hence, it is the Bajrāchāryas more than any others who will be able to perform such aniconic worship.

2. The pīṭhapūjā

2.1 Preliminary remarks

The *pīṭhapūjā* consists in a visit to places which are considered the seats of the Mother Goddesses (*Mātṛkās*), who are eight in number. In their *pīṭhas,* they usually manifest themselves in the shape of unhewn stones. Their sanctuaries may be open shrines, without a building being erected over them, just the delimination being marked (Fig. 3, 4); again, at times a *Mātṛkā* will be housed in a pagoda of up to three roofs (Fig. 2) : in that case, the sanctuary is usually closed at the sides.

2. Joseph Rykwert; *The Idea of a Town; in: Forum voor Architectuur en daarmee verbonden Kunsten;* No. 3, Hilversum 1963, *p.* 99–148
———; *The Idea of a Town–The anthropolgy in Urban form in Rome/Italy and the Ancient World;* 1976
Rykwert suggested, that the cosmological structure of ritual represents 'an irreducible element, an atom of human experience' (p. 139)

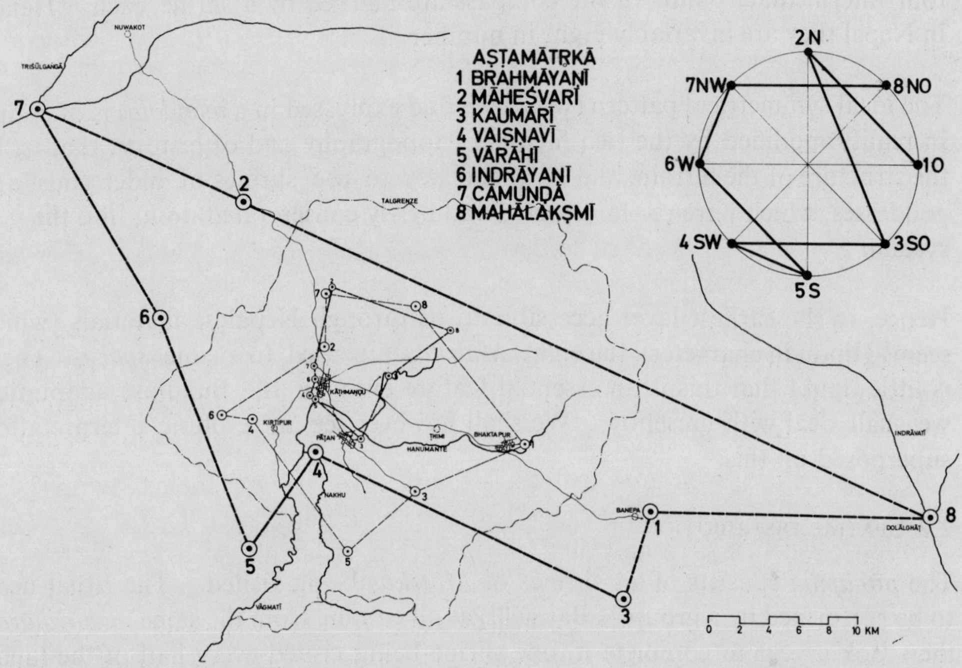

Fig. 1

Valley of Kāṭhmāṇḍu : location of the 24 *mātṛkā pīṭhas* around the city of Kāṭhmāṇḍu, where the Bajrācārya lives, who performs the *caturviṃśatipīṭhapūjā* within one year. The places of worship form three circles or maṇḍalas, which are characterized by the terms *cittacakra, vākcakra* and *kāyacakra*. These belong to the concepts of Tantrik Buddhism.

Mātṛkās are one of the most essential, and indeed most frequent, devices for the sanctification of Nepalese towns[3]. Preferably they are arranged so as to surround settlements – ideally in a pattern where the four cardinal and the four intermediate points of the compass are marked by a shrine each. Hence, in Nepal they are invariably eight in number.

The ideal symmetrical pattern (which we find expressed in a *maṇḍala*) is of course in reality modified by the two factors of topography and of history: that is, by the structure of the terrain, and by a tendency to use shrines of older gods and goddesses, which were re– interpreted and newly consercrated, to fit into the new system.

Hence, in the earliest layer accessible to us through Nepalese materials (which seems Hindu in character), the eight *Mātṛkās* are used to define *space*. There is little doubt that this is an essential feature even in the Buddhist adaptation we shall deal with presently. We shall however see an esoteric interpretation superposed on this.

2.2 Spatial distribution

The *pīṭhapūjā* consists of 24 shrines of *Mātṛkās* being visited. The ritual used to be performed by a group of Bajrācāryas all coming from the same *mahāvihāra;* they took a year to complete it, one shrine being visited every half of the lunar month.

The 24 shrines are arranged in three sets of eight *Mātṛkās* each : the same sequence of *Mātṛkās* is affirmed to exist in three separate and widening circles.

First of all, let us look at topography. The first of these circles by and large surrounds the city of Kāṭhmāṇḍu, the second the entire valley, and the third at times transcends the boundaries of the valley proper to include places traditionally under the spiritual – and at most times also secular – domination of Newar kings.

3. For the significance of the *Aṣṭamātṛkā* in connection with urban space see:
N. Gutschow, B. Kölver; *Ordered Space – Concepts and Functions in a Town in Nepal;* Wiesbaden 1975
B. Kölver; *A Ritual Map from Nepal;* in: Folia Rara (Festschrift W. Voigt), Wiesbaden 1976
J. Pieper; *Three Cities of Nepal;* in: *Shelter, Sign & Symbol,* ed. by Paul Oliver; London 1975, p. 52–70

Fig. 2
Kathmandu : Camunda pith (also called Luti Ajima) at the banks of Bisnumati (Nr. 7, northwest of *cittacakra*).
The goddess is represented by an unhewn stone in the open groundfloor, looking northwards. The three tiered pagoda serves to mark the sacred place. Several smaller buildings (*pauva*) serve as shelter for those who attend the *puja* or a cremation at the nearby Masan Ghat.

Fig. 3
Gokarna : Mahalaksmi pith (also called Gokarnesvari) at the banks of Bagmati, north of the village of Gokarna (No. 8, northeast of *cittacakra*). The sacred place is only marked by an one-storeyed open structure (*pauva*). The roof is already falling apart, signalizing growing neglect of place and ritual.

As for the *first circle,* this extends from Guhyeśvarī and Gokarṇa in the east up to the banks of the Biṣṇumatī in the west, including a shrine from Pāṭan (*Balkaumārī*), which is, in another context, the seat of one of the *Aṣṭamātṛkā* of Pāṭan.[4] The *second polygon* is made up of sanctuaries farther away from the centre : we find the easternmost of the Bhaktapur *Mātṛkās* (*Brahmāyaṇī*) just as shrines of smaller Newar settlements such as Lubhu (*Kaumārī*) and Sattungal (*Indrāyaṇī*).

The *third circle* spans the wide gap between the two groups of Seven Rivers (Saptakauśikī and Saptagaṇḍakī)[5] which encase the heart of Nepal : its *Mahālakṣmī* is found far east at the confluence of Indravatī and the Sunkośī Rivers, in the north west we find *Cāmuṇḍā* at the confluence of Triśulgaṅgā and Tadhikola. The two important Newar settlements outside the valley, Panauti and Banepa, are also visited in this cirle.

Up to this point, the system is not essentially different from that preserved in traditional, pseudo-historical accounts, the so-called *Vamśāvalīs:* these contain similar repeated systems of *Aṣṭamātṛkās* which indicate the sanctification of successive units : first the capital, then the Valley, then the entire Kingdom.[6]

The Bajrācārya *pīṭhapūjā,* however, differs from those in one essential respect : the shrines visited were not installed with this particular *pūjā* in mind. The connection between the three systems of eight shrines each only exists in the minds and in the acts of those who perform the ritual; there is no visual trace which would make the system evident to the uninitiated. Again : the system is realized only in time, in its actual performance.[7] Certain places are assembled to form an imaginary *maṇḍala :* and the fact that this *maṇḍala* is hidden from the eye of the uninitiated vouches for its significance, 'for', as the Bṛhad-āraṇyaka-upaniṣad says, 'the gods as it were love what is hidden' (*parokṣapriyā iva hi devāḥ,* BĀU 4, 2, 2).

4. It seems strange to see No. 6 of *cittacakra* noted as *Indrāyaṇī* and No. 7 as *Cāmuṇḍā,* although in the context of the City *Aṣṭamātṛkās* it is the other way round.
5. *Bhāṣāvaṃśāvalī* 1, Kāṭhmāṇḍu 2020 V.S., p. 41 or: A. *Oldfield: Sketches of Nipal,* Vol, I: London 1880; p. 27
6. *Bhāṣāvaṃśāvalī* 1, Kāṭhmāṇḍu 2020 V.S., p. 31
7. E. v. Erodberg-Consten; *Zeit und Raum in der Geomantik;* in: *Stadt und Landschaft – Raum und Zeit,* Festschrift für Erich Kühn; Köln 1969 An excellent account on interrelations of symbols for time and space. Were the *piṭhapūjā* not performed in Buddhist context we would have dealt with interpretations based on the number 24 representing the 24 sections of the solar year.

Fig. 4.
Gokarṇa : Mahālakṣmī pīṭh. The goddes (*mātṛkā*) is represented by a row of ten unhewn stones, showing marks (colour) of ritual use.

3. Patterns of interpretation

We will now have to try and understand the significance of the ritual. This attempt cannot be more than a first approximation.

We have seen how on the most elementary and transparent level the ritual defines the territory which is the home of the worshipper, the home of his creed. The interpretation which the Bajrācārya will consider more important, however, is hinted at by the three terms which serve to characterize the three *mandalas*: these are *cittacakra, vākcakra* and *kāyacakra*. These terms belong to the concepts of Tantrik Buddhism.

Tantrik thought is based upon Sāṃkhya philosophy, which departs from a fundamental distinction, that between soul and matter (*puruṣa* and *prakṛti*). Matter consists of 24 substances (*tattvas*) of ever grosser structure. Both the human body and the world outside are composed of these 24 substances : hence to the initiated, the distinction between the outside world and the self is, as it where, resolved : both of them are made up of the same components, both illustrate the same principles, hence mastery over the self – which at the highest stage culminates in the resolution of individual existence– is achieved by conscious control over the human body, i. e. the substances or elements it consists of – and recognizing these elements is a first and essential step in this process.

Here, then , is a second plane which is symbolized by the vistit to the 24 Mothers : they stand for the 24 elements (*tattvas*) of the world and of the human body.

(Note: the 25th element of Sāṃkhya philosphy, the soul (*puruṣa*) of course does not occur in a Buddhist context).

Now, according to Tantrik teaching the body holds a number of nerve centres, plexuses, *cakras* (as the Sanskrit term goes), which are of particular importance in the process of achieving mastery over the body. Hindu Tantras lists seven such *cakras*.[8] When the Buddhists came to reflect upon this system, they identified these cakras of the body with the 'Three Bodies' (*trikāya*) of the Buddha.[9] Although these stem from an altogether different source, they determined the Buddhist version of the list of the *cakras* within the body. Thus, some Buddhist Tantras distinguish between three *cakras* ; the Hevajratantra says that there is a lowest *cakra* close to the heart, a second one in the throat, and a third one in the head.

8. Shashi Bhushan DAS GUPTA; *An Introduction to Tantric Buddhism.* (Sec. Ed.), Berkeley and London 1974, pp. 146–153
9. A.K. WARDER; *Indian Buddhism;* New Delhi 1970, pp. 412

In the three designations of its *cakras,* the Bajrācārya ritual obviously refers to this system. The *first* and outermost *circle,* the *kāyacakra* 'circle of body', is located in the region of the forehead and corresponds to the *nirmāṇakāya* of the Buddha, i. e. his corporeal aspect : it stands for the Buddha or Bhuddhas as they appear in human guise : they are a mere reflection of the Buddha principle.

The *second cakra* is in the works of the Bajrācārya called *vākcakra* 'circle of word or speech' : it is located in the throat and stands for the *saṃbhogakāya* of the Buddha, i.e. for the Buddha when he appears as the 'King of the Doctrine'; if we stick to the image contained in the words 'throat' or 'speech', we are justified to say the Bajrācārya refers to the teachings of the Buddha, such as they have been uttered.

The highest, *innermost circle* is to the Bajrācārya, *cittacakra* the '*cakra* of thought': this signifies the *svabhāvakāya* or *dharmakāya* of the Buddha, i. e. the proper and true Nature of Things, far beyond the confusing and indeed misleading world of phenomena : permanent and immoveable, it is in a sense the Perfection of Wisdom which is the (unspeakable) essence of Buddhist thought.

Let us not forget that applying the theory of the nerve centres to the aspects of the Buddha is but one of the interpretations this system can be subjected to. It is just as correct, just as orthodox, to apply it to the human body : that is, to the three realms of the senses, of speech (taken as the embodiment of thought), and of Highest Bliss or Highest Truth, which a person will reach when he has mastered the preceeding stages–and which he will variously define, as Emptiness, or as Perfection of Wisdom.

Again : on one plane we can say the Bajrācārya affirms that his country stands for the three ways in which the Buddha and his teachings become manifest in the world. On another plane : his pilgrimage makes him realize how the world he inhabits, the world characterized by Newar culture, is mirrored in his body, is identiacal with it. It is very secular, very Western to take this idea as an image, as a symbol of how a human being is embedded in his culture, is rooted in his soil : yet this is true, though this could be considered a very superficial and indeed marginal interpretation of what the Bajrācārya is doing. And the very image can be turned the other way round, without loosing its truth or value: his way outside, his visit to the *pīṭhas,* is a way into his own self: the essence of his own physical and psychical structure very directly stands for the country he lives in, stands for the essence of the doctrine he follows.

Outside of Hindu or Buddhist culture, it will be hard to find a similar instance of intellectual subtlety and complexity being translated into a symbol of direct appeal.

Appendix :

Direction, name and location of the 24 mātṛkā. – *Caturviṁśati Pīṭha*

1. Circle – Prathama cittacakra-mātṛkā

1.	1. *pūrva* (E)	:	Brahmāyaṇī	pīṭh	(Guhyeśvarī)	Paśupati – Sāntatīrtha
2.	2. *uttara* (N)	:	Maheśvarī	pīṭh	(Manamaijū)	Tokhā-Manorathatīrtha
3.	3. *agni* (SE)	:	Kaumārī	pīṭh	(Śaṃkareśvarī)	Śaṃkhamūla – Śaṃkarathīrtha
4.	4. *nairṛtya* (SW)	:	Vaiṣṇavī	pīṭh	(Jñaneśvarī)	Karha Khusī – Jñanatīrtha
5.	5. *dakṣiṇa* (S)	:	Vārāhī	pīṭh	(Majyeśvarī)	Bāgmatī-Pacalī Rājatīrtha
6.	6. *paścima* (W)	:	Indrāyaṇī	pīṭh	(Kaṃkeśvarī)	Bisṇumatī – Lakhutīrtha
7.	7. *vāyavya* (NW)	:	Cāmuṇḍā	pīṭh	(Lutī Ajimā)	Bhacā Khusī – Nirmalatīrtha
8.	8. *īśāna* (NE)	:	Mahālakṣmī	pīṭh	(Goṛkarṇeśvarī)	Gokarṇa – Puṇyatīrtha

2. Circle – Dvitīya vākcakra-mātṛkā

9.	1. *pūrva* (E)	:	Brahmāyaṇī	pīṭh	Khopayāpine Vantāṃkṣetra
10.	2. *uttara* (N)	:	Maheśvarī	pīṭh	Mhayepī (near Balajū)
11.	3. *agni* (SE)	:	Kaumārī	pīṭh	Lubhu
12.	4. *nairṛtya* (SW)	:	Vaiṣṇavī	pīṭh	Balakhu Khusī (south of Kīrtipur)
13.	5. *dakṣiṇa* (S)	:	Vajravārāhī	pīṭh	Wādeśa (Cāpāgāum)
14.	6. *paścima* (W)	:	Indrāyaṇī	pīṭh	Sattuṃgala
15.	7. *vāyavya* (NW)	:	Cāmuṇḍā	pīṭh	Phusīṃkhyaḥ
16.	8. *iśāna* (NE)	:	Mahālakṣmī	pīṭh	Kantināmadeśa

3. Circle – Tritīya kāyacakra-mātṛkā

17.	1. *pūrva* (E)	:	Brahmāyaṇī	pīṭh	Bhoṃta Caṇḍeśvarī (Banepā)
18.	2. *uttara* (N)	:	Maheśvarī	pīṭh	Kapilāsa
19.	3. *agni* (SE)	:	Kaumārī	pīṭh	Panautī
20.	4. *nairṛtya* (SW)	:	Vaiṣṇavī	pīṭh	Yappā (south of Pāṭan)
21.	5. *dakṣiṇa* (S)	:	Vārāhī	pīṭh	Dakṣiṇa Kālī
22.	6. *paścima* (W)	:	Indrāyaṇī	pīṭh	Gokhudeśa
23.	7. *vāyavya* (NW)	:	Cāmuṇḍā	pīṭh	Triśulī Devīghāṭ (near Nuwākoṭ)
24.	8. *īśāna* (NE)	:	Mahālakṣmī	pīṭh	Dolālghāṭ

Dolpo–The Highest Settlement Area in Western Nepal

Christian Kleinert

INTRQDUCTION.

Nepal is among the countries with the highest settlements. Dolpo, the most elevated area in Western Nepal settled throughout the year (Charka, 4350 m.= 14272 feet) is one of the least accessible parts of the Nepal Himalayas. The roads linking it with Tibet and with the neighbouring areas of Nepal have the disadvantage of several high passes which remain snow-covered until late spring. The routes along the gorges of the Bheri and of the Langu Khola – the two rivers in which the water resources of the area drain away–are either in bad repair and are not passable for pack animals (Bheri) or they are open only for a few weeks per year (Langu), when the low level of the water in winter will allow a multiple crossing of the stream (ref., pl. 2).

Due to the remoteness of the area, only a few scientists and some mountaineering expeditions have come to Dolpo[1]. Very little, accordingly, has been published, and researches were concentrated mainly on botanical, ethnological, religious and geological themes. Nothing has, however, been published so far on the housing and settlement patterns in that area.

During my two years of research in Nepal,[2] I stayed in Dolpo twice. While taking a round journey of the Dhaulagiri Himal in the spring and the summer of 1970, I visited the southern and the eastern parts of Dolpo in May and June, 1970. During the spring 1971, I could also see the northern part of Dolpo, when I went from the North-Western border areas of Nepal (Humla, Mugu) to Thak Khola. The survey on settlement patterns in my earlier book "THE HOUSING AND SETTLEMENT PATTERNS IN THE NEPAL-HIMALAYA, WITH SPECIAL REFERENCE TO CLIMATIC FACTORS"[3] (in German), contains a few remarks on the village patterns and the forms of houses in Dolpo, too.

1) TICHY (1953), TUCCI (1952) HAGEN (1954), SNELLGROVE (1956 and 1960/61), POLUNIN (1952), FUCHS (1963), FÜRER-HAIMENDORF (1962) JEST, AUFSCHNAITER (several journeys).

2) With a scholarship of the DAAD (German Academic Exchange Service), September 1969 to July 1971.

3) I should like to thank Peter AUFSCHNAITER, Kathmandu Dr. Dolf NOORDIJK, Warmond, and John TYSON, (Rugby) for informations on the areas visited, and also Prof. Dr. Christoph v. FÜRER-HAIMENDORF, London, and Dor Bahadur BISTA, Kathmandu.

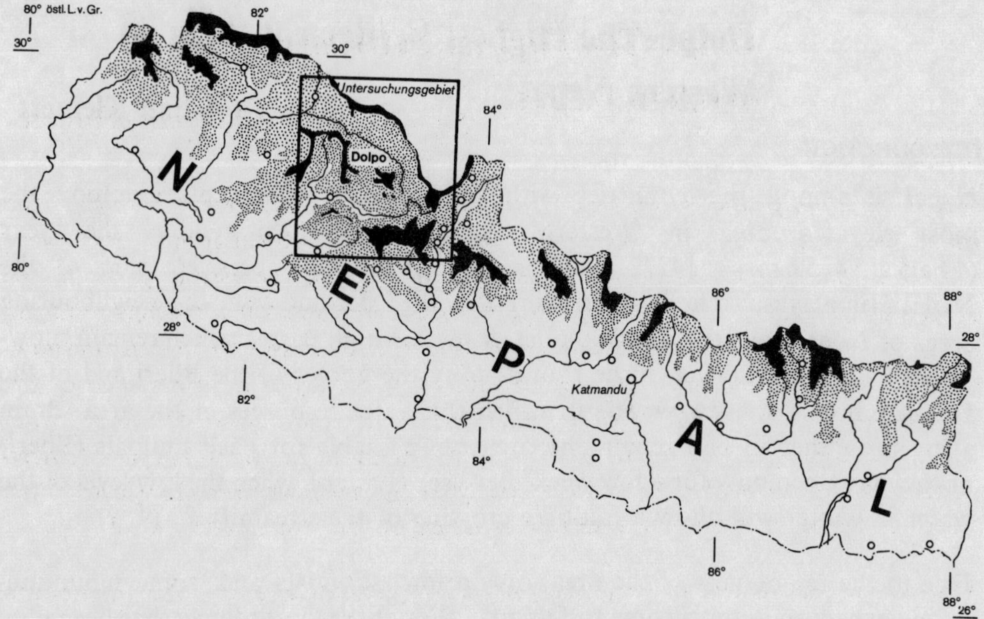

PLATE 1 Situation of the are investigated. MARTEN's Map has been used for the preparation of this sketch. Altitudes according to the quarter inch maps of the Survey of India.

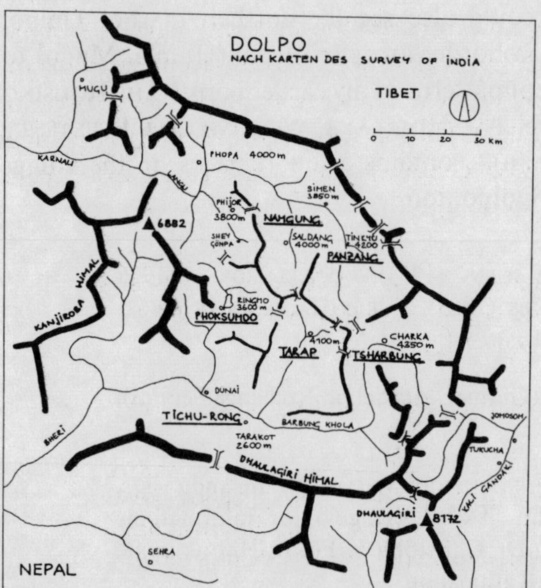

PLATE 2 Dolpo and neighbouring areas.

ENVIRONMENTAL AND ECONOMIC CONDITIONS OF THE AREA

The area investigated here is surrounded with high mountain ranges on all sides. In the south it is the range of the Dhaulagiri Himal with one peak of some 8000 m. and several of some 7000 m. altitude. In the west, there is the Kanjiroba Himal, in the north and north-east the mountains on the Tibetan border, in the east the Mukut Himal (ref., pl. 2).

According to SNELLGROVE, Dolpo proper is formed by the districts of Namgung, Panzang, Tsharbung and Tarap[4]. These areas are situated at an average altitude of 4000 to 5000 m., the settlements are to be found between 3400 m. (Terang) and 4350 m. (Charka).

The areas bordering Central Dolpo in the South-West (i.e. Phoksumdo and Tichu Rong), have got a lower altitude than the four central districts and they also differ in the composition of their population as well as in the economic pursuits.

CLIMATIC CONDITIONS

The climatic conditions of this area can only be judged properly by taking into account the state of vegetation, the reports of weather stations from the neighbouring areas, and personal observations of the area to be investigated. All over Dolpo there is no weather station until now. The neighbouring stations have reported the following data (for the location of the station, ref., ill. 2).

Table 1 : Climatical reports of the weather stations bordering Dolpo (according to "Climatological Records of Nepal")

Station	Elevation in metre	Yearly average rainfall in mm	Average temp. in January C°	Average temp. in July C°
Jomosom	2800 m.	270 mm.	4, 5	19, 5
Dunai	2803 m.	1170 mm.	not reported	not reported
Mugu	3787 m.	1286 mm.	" "	" "
Sehra	2046 m.	1340 mm.	" "	" "

4) This demarcation is made according to the definition of the Dolpo people and does not coincide with the political boundaries, introduced by HMG, according to which the areas of Tichu Rong and Phoksumdo, too, with the district headquarters at Dunai, belong to the "Dolpa" region.

Only one of the stations in table 1, i.e. Dunai, is situated in the (political division) of Dolpo Zilla. The reports, however, create some doubts in regard to their accuracy: The data of Dunai show a rainfall of 2486 mm. per annum in 1965. The high altitude areas of Dolpo, with the main settlement areas at an altitude of some 4000 m., are not covered by these data. The climate of this area is much more severe due to the extreme altitude. Except for the few months of summer, severe night frost is met with throughout the year. The seasonal change of climate from a mild influence of the summer monsoon, which is apparent in the summer months with slight drizzle from a often cloudy sky, to the dry season of winter results in relatively warm summer with little change in temperature on one hand, and in an extremely dry period lasting from the end of September to the end of May.

In winter, temperatures generally remain below freezing point all day long.[5] The average rainfall in Jomosom 270 mm., (situated in the Thak Khola, east of Dolpo), is the lowest one recorded in the entire Nepal, and is typical for the conditions of the areas north of the Great Himalayan Range sheltered from rain by ca. 8000 m. high Annapurna and Dhaulagiri (ref., ill. 2). The data of the Dolpo area, which is not that much protected from monsoon influence, must be somewhat higher and can be assumed to be around 500 mm. per annum.

VEGETATION

This assumption is warranted by the actual conditions of the vegetation met with. Conditions similar to the semi-deserted valley bottom of the upper Kali Gandaki, which is situated eastward of Dolpo, are found only at the bottom of the valleys of Barbung Khola and Panzang Chu (upper Karnali), according to the vegetation map of DOBREMEZ[6]. In these areas as well as in the upper Karnali Valley, humidity increases with altitude so much that the upper slopes and the water head areas of the valleys at an altitude of ca. 4500 m. are covered by far spread alpine pastures, which are intensively used for cattle grazing during the monsoon period.

The whole Dolpo settlement area is situated above the treeline except for a few

5) According to own observations in the area described here, and according to local information.

6) JEST and DOMBREMEZ (1969) : extreme 'alpine steppe' at the bottom of the valley around Phijor and Simen.

7) PINUS EXCELSA and BETULA UTILIS at an altitude of more than 4200 m., near Shey Gompa and along the Barbung Khola between Terang and Mukut.

Ill. 1 Tarakot (2600 m.) situated on a spur some 200 m. above the valley bottom of the Barbung Khola, which drains away the water from the Northern side of Dhaulagiri Himal.

Ill. 2 House in Saldang (4 100.) Branches of bushes along the rims of the roof used as fuel. In the foreground, a chorten with mani wall. Alpine scrub around Saldang, only a few willows along the water courses. Barley on the fields.

insular patches of wood, being the most elevated spots of the thin subalpine belt of woods. Wood for house construction, therefore, has to be carried in a several days' trip from the wooded areas of Phoksumdo –Lake or from the Lower Tarap and Barbung Khola (ref., ill. 2). Dried yak dung as well as dry branches, taken from the bushes of the alpine "steppes", is used for fuel.

Population

The four districts of Dolpo proper are inhabited by pure Tibetans (Bhotes). One has to distinguish between the Bhotes settled in these areas since long, and the Tibetan refugees who only came after the Chinese occupation of Tibet, and especially in 1959/60, after the revolt in Tibet. While the Bhotes of Dolpo, settled there since long, are living in villages, and are engaged in cattle breeding, agriculture and trade with Tibet, most of the Tibetan refugees live in tents outside the villages during the whole year and subsist on cattle breeding only. The population of the areas bordering Dolpo in the South-West i.e. Phoksumdo and Tichu Rong, are designated by Jest (1969, p. 189) as 'Tibetan' or 'Tibeto-Burmese' regarding their language, and as Buddhists, with respect to their religion. This, however, does not say anything about the ethnical classification of this population. Snellgrove (1961, pp. 36 and 61), calls the inhabitants of the Phoksumdo area and of Tichu Rong a mixed population of Magars and Tibetans, the degree of their 'Tibetanization' being only evident by their exclusive use of the Tibetan language and their adherance to Lamaist Buddhism of Tibetan brand.

Economy

The economic basis, i.e. agriculture, cattle breeding and trade, to a great extent is the result of the conditions of nature prevailing in the area.

Agriculture, i.e. cultivation of irrigated land, can be found up to an altitude of some 4400 m. The highest fields are those of Namgung (4400 m.), west of Saldang), Senting (4450 m., Barbung Khola) and Charka (4350 m.)[8]. The irrigation of the terraced fields and the channels running along the contour-lines characterizes the cultivated land. In high Dolpo proper, this is a genuine oasis cultivation, while in Phoksumdo and Tichu Rong, monsoon cultivation (without irrigation) is possible due to higher precipitation and lower altitude. Only barley is being grown in the higher altitudes, although potato would thrive because of climatic conditions favourable for it. In the area of Phoksumdo and Tichu Rong, wheat and buck wheat are grown, too. Due to the lower altitude of Tichu Rong two harvests per year are possible.

8) All altitudes are according to the new one inch to one mile map of the Survey of India, converted from feet to metres.

Cattle breeding plays a dominant role in the high altitude areas of Dolpo. The Yak contributes milk, meat and wool. It is also an indispensable pack animal. In an epidemic, brought to Dolpo by Yaks of Tibetan refugees, the number of animals was temporarily decimated severely, after 1960. In the meantime, the situation has improved again. Besides Yaks, there are also big herds of sheep and goats.

In summer, the herds are taken to alpine pastures situated at an altitude of 4200–4700 m. The weak influence of the monsoon results in the development of an alpine meadow belt at this elevation. Traditionally, in winter the herds had been brought to the pastures along the Tsangpo (upper Brahmaputra) in Tibet.
Since the Chinese occupation of Tibet, however, these pastures can no longer be used. Some parts of the herd are now being taken via the passes in the West (Numa La 5100 m. and Kagmara La 5050 m.), to the high altitude pastures south of Kanjiroba Himal, which are not used in winter by the Chetri-Thakuri, an Indo-Nepalese population, living in that area.[9]

TRADE

The situation of Dolpo as a border area has been favourable to trade between Tibet and the countries south of the Himalayas, that has been carried out by the Dolpo Bhotes since ancient times. After a lull which lasted some ten years (1960–1970), following the revolt in Tibet, trade has been resumed to a greater extent. The main reason for this seems to be the requirements of the Chinese Administration in Tibet, especially of rice and sugar. This favours a small scale border crossing trade by the inhabitants of Dolpo as well as by those of other Nepalese areas along the Himalayan border. Mainly rice and sugar brought from south of the Great Himalayan Range are exchanged for salt and wool from Tibet. The re-orientation of winter quarters for Dolpo cattle from the pastures in Tibet to the lower lying Nepalese area bordering Dolpo in the South-West has also resulted in more contacts of the Doplo people with the South. Today, hens and other goods from the Nepalese hills are found in almost every Dolpo village, which had been a rare thing a few years ago.

9) The Indo-Aryan groups prefer the warmer areas of the Southern slopes of the Himalaya, and do not settle above 3000 m., in other areas of Nepal (East and Central Nepal) not even above 2000 m., while the Tibetans prefer the higher altitudes. The high lying pastures on the Southern slopes, therefore, are used by Chettris and Thakuris only in summer, and are open to Dolpo people in winter.

Winter is the trading season, in which the low lying areas in the south of Dolpo are visited. Tibetans dislike the summer-heat of the areas south of the Himalayas.

Trade with Ṭibet, however, is carried out during the summer, when the passes, generally at an altitude of more than 5000 m., are not covered with snow. Blankets and clothing are produced from handspun wool in Dolpo homes by using very simple looms. A part of these products is sold or exchanged for rice and sugar on the markets south of the Great Himalayan Range (ref., ill. 5).

House and Settlement

Houses and settlements in Dolpo are adapted to natural conditions, as in all other parts of the Nepal Himalaya. The high degree of isolation of these settlements in the Inner Himalayas resulted in a type of house construction which makes use of local building materials only. The houses, therefore, seem to have grown from the landscape itself (ref., pl. 2).

Pattern of House Construction

The rough climate of the mountains, with its severe winters, the big difference of temperature between day and night because of the arid conditions, the intensive sunlight caused by high altitude, and the utmost decrease of warmth at night, have resulted in a very compact type of house construction. The characteristics of the materials used for construction suit the stress of climatic conditions to a great extent.

Thick walls, made of crudely dressed stone or mud mortar, provide necessary protection against the cold winter. There are no windows, or only a few ones. The only other openings are the front door, and a hole in the ailing as access to the flat roof and to let out the smoke. The thick walls, made from the above-mentioned materials, due to susceptibility of absorption of warmth or cold, can withstand the big differences in temperature caused by heating of the materials in day-time and cooling at night. The type of house—a closed cube with flat roofs made from mud or mud mortar—is a pattern found in all other areas with arid climate. Good wood for construction is very rare due to the meagre vegetation in these high altitude areas. Therefore, the outer appearance of the houses is characterized totally by the unplastered materials used for wall construction (natural stone and mud concrete). Only the living rooms of especially wealthy people have a wooden flooring. In comparision to other areas of the Inner Nepal Himalaya, the interior furnishing with wooden cupboards and shelves is poor. Carefully guarded piles of wood on the rims of the roofs are preserved for the use during the winter. At the same time, these piles serve as roof terrace walls and as a protection against wind (ref., ill. 2).

PLATE 3

SALDANG, DOLPO
4000 m

1 House
2 Store
3 Stable

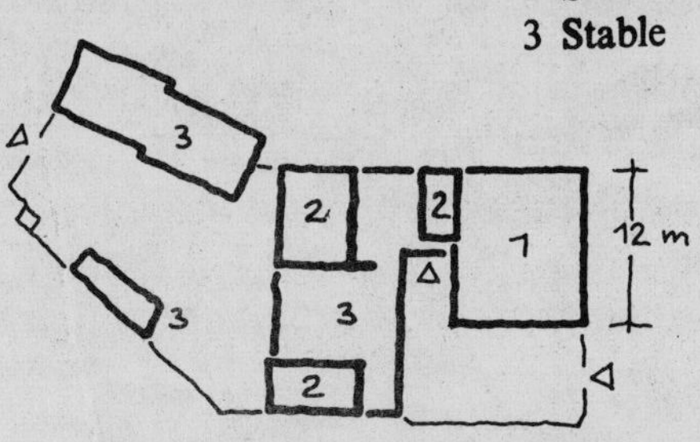

Layout of the house of Labrang Tensing.

Ringmo, Phoksumdo Lake, 3600 m.

Residential house

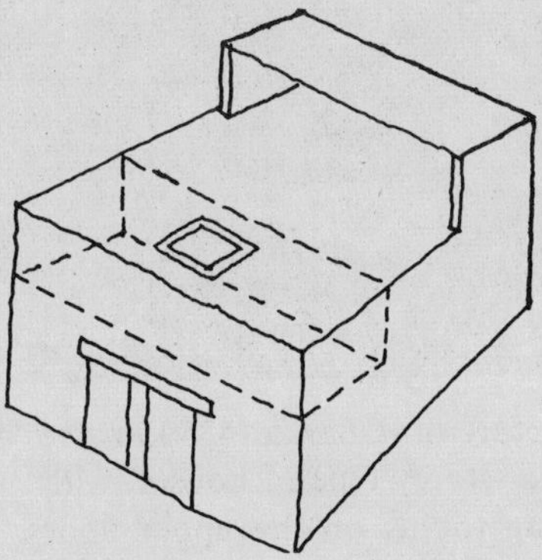

Living room in the upper floor

Monastery

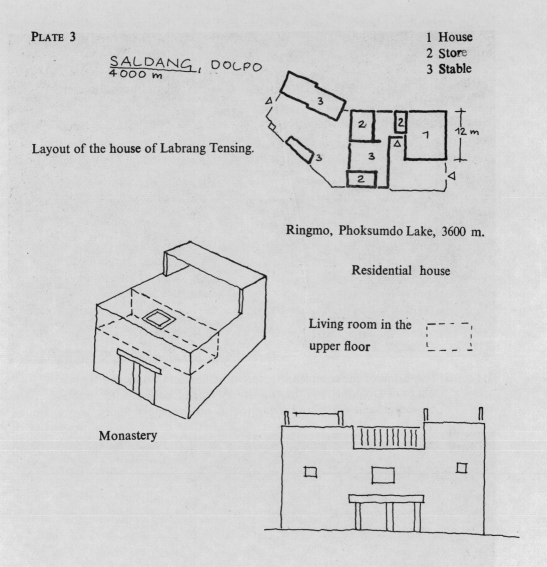

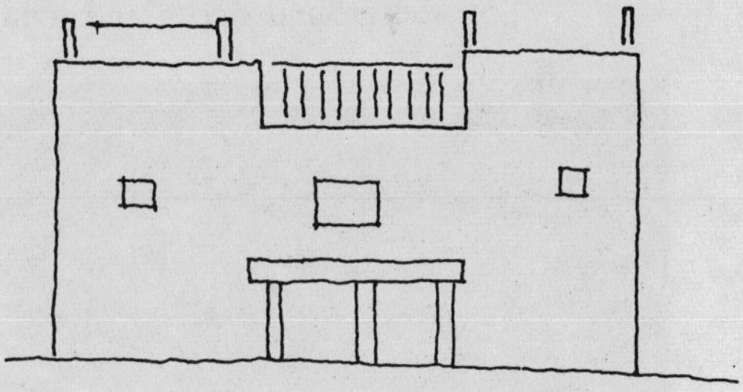

GROUND PLAN OF THE HOUSES

Houses in Dolpo consist of two storeys: stables on the ground floor and living rooms in the upper storey– a pattern found in most parts of the Nepal Himalaya. On top of the roofs there often is a partly open, partly closed storey covering only half of the roof. Here harvest and stores are kept. The central courtyards in the middle of the actual living area, which are frequently met within neighbouring regions[10], are but little developed in Dolpo, and are mostly restricted to big openings leading to the roof. The large central living-room on

10) Especially in Thak Khola used as protective measure against the high velocity of winds in the Kali Gandaki valley.

Ill. 3 This detail of the complex structure of Charka (4350 m. the highest village of Dolpo) shows the two -storey-type of houses, with stables on the ground floors and living rooms on the upper floors.

Ill. 4 Tinkyu (4200 m). Upper part of the village, with the cultuivated areas on the low marshy land of a Northern tributary river. The village is situated immediately below a pass leading to Tibet. Even nowadays, trading salt is important for the local population.

the upper floor is the centre of the family life which is concentrated around the open fire– almost never allowed to be extinguished. During the winter, the villages often are blocked by snow for months. Then activities are completely withdrawn to the bunkerlike houses around the open fire. The living area is protected from the cold ground by stables on the ground floor and their animal warmth. Store rooms and some additional rooms are attached to the main living room. These are mostly without any windows at all. Courtyards for cattle and agricultural processing, which are connected with the main house by walls, form a compact, fortresslike unit of the various houses and added farm buildings.

SETTLEMENT PATTERN

The location of the settlements is a result of the relief and of the natural conditions prevailing for irrigation of the fields. The settlements along the Barbung Khola, for instance, are situated on flat terraces of south facing slopes, up to 1000 m. above the gorgelike narrow bottom of the valley. These places are the most favourable ones for settlement. These villages are real oasises, situated close to springs or small tributary rivers the water of which can be used for the irrigation of the fields. The desertlike, arid bottom of the Barbung Khola Valley is completely uninhabited. In the villages situated on Southern slopes, which are exposed to extreme dryness (like Pimring, Ghiring and Terang[11]) the water is usually collected in small reservoirs at night and distributed to the fields at day-time (ref., ill. 1).

In the high altitude areas along the upper courses of the two rivers catching the waters of Dolpo, the formation of the ground often is gentle and thus, favourable for settlements and agriculture even close to the rivers. Frequently, the settlements are situated below the confluence of a tributary river, the water of which is diverted by channels and used for irrigation (ref., ill. 3).

The pattern of the settlements is not uniform. There are single houses widely dispersed over the fields, while the unit of a house and courtyard is very compact (ref., ill. 2). Frequently, however, the scarcity of arable land leads to a very compact village pattern: arable land which can be irrigated is not occupied by buildings at all. The areas remaining for construction are extremely densely built on. Often all houses of a village form a single building (ref., ill. 4).

The advantage of such a settlement pattern is to provide a special protection against the severe climate of the high mountain areas. Such houses have got only minimal outward walls in order to keep the warmth instead of cooling down rapidly. There is not much surface for winter storms to attack these

11) The system spelling the names of villages, follows the one employed in the maps of the Survey of India, which is not always identical with Tibetan pronunciation.

Ill. 5 Gate chorten and mani walls at the entrance to the village of Namdo, Namgung (4100 m.) in the back ground, the mountain range which has to be crossed via passes leading to Tarap and the Phoksumdo Lake.

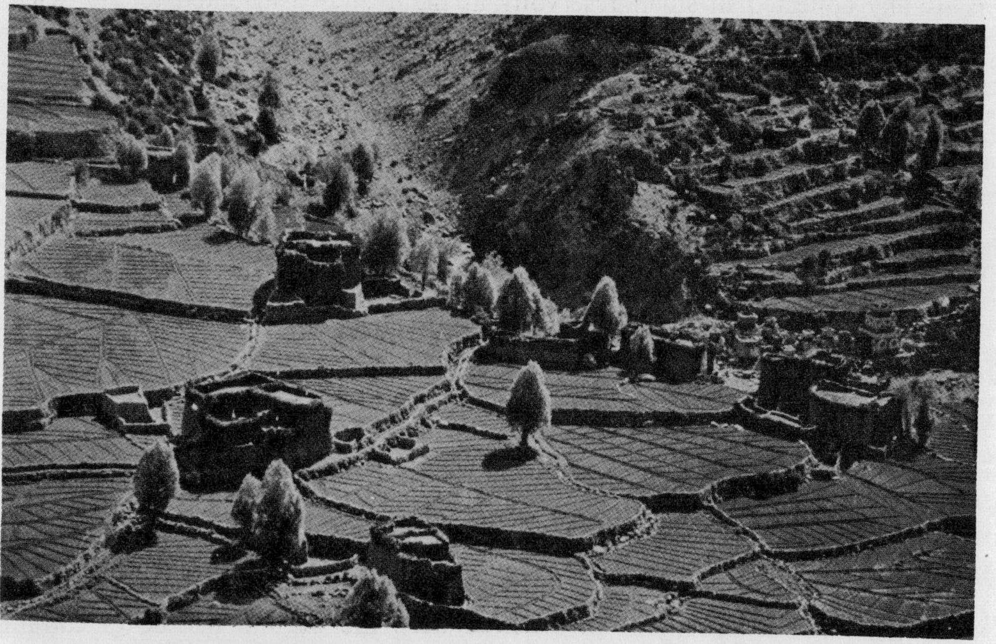

Ill. 6 Village of Simen (3850 m.). The various houses are scattered all over the cultivated land. The photo shows the minuitely ramified system of irrigation channels running through the fields. Along the main water courses, willows. Summer barley as the only crop.

houses. As described above with regard to single houses, in these compact villages, all houses, courtyards, farm buildings form a single, fortresslike unit. During the winter, the people live in the village together with the cattle: Animal warmth is as welcome as dried dung, which is used as additional fuel.

The settlement patterns of Dolpo are to be traced back to Tibetan origin. It is remarkable that the villages with the most closely built pattern, are to be found just before the passes leading from Dolpo to neighbouring areas (Charka, Tarakot). Frequently, the name of the village (Tibet.- *Dzong-* "fort"), and the location at strategically important points indicate that these had been fortresses, dating back to the time of autonomous Tibetan principalities of this area.

Abandoned fields and a great number of ruins are testimony of an earlier *Period of Abandonment.* Big terraced slopes which are no longer used and ruined houses at Tinkyu, Karma and Phijor, indicate that agriculture and number of population are decreasing. Toni HAGEN (1971 p. 83) explains the depopulation of the valleys of the Inner Himalayas by a deterioration of climate in the Northern Himalaya, which until now has not yet been investigated properly. It is still unknown, when the process of abandonment took place. At present, there are no indications, that a further depopulation of the villages of Dolpo is underway, (ref., ill. 4).

The influence of Buddhist religion is to be seen in the demarcation of the boundaries of the villages by long rows of Mani walls, with hundreds of Mani stones,[12] and by gate-Chortens (small turrets with prayer wheels), through which you enter the village (ref., ill. 5). The Mani stones are votive presents which serve to gain religious merit. They are in flat reliefs and show inscriptions or figurative representations. Mani walls and Chortens form the outer boundary of a village. Single houses are rarely found outside the village demarcated by these sacred buildings. Every house, however, has got some flag poles to which prayer flags are attached. These strongly influence the outward appearance of a settlement.

Monasteries are either situated as village temple inside the village, or also outside, as recluses or separate monastic settlements (Shey Gompa, Samling). Shey Gompa is the main Lamaistic monastery of Dolpo. Samling is the main Bon monastery, belonging to this pre-Lamaistic religion which has survived only in a few retreat areas of difficult access.

12) A kind of votive boards, to be found in all Buddhist areas of Nepal.

LITERATURE

FÜRER-HAIMENDORF, CH. : Himalayan Traders, London 1975.

HAGEN, T. : Nepal, Königreich am Himalaya, Second edition, Bern 1971.

JEST, C., and DOBREMEZ, J.F.: Carte Ecologique de la Region Annapurna-Dhaulagiri, Paris–Grenoble 1969.

JEST, C. : Traditions et Croyances Religieuses des Habitants de la Vallée de Tichu-Rong (Nord-ouest du Népal); in: L'Ethnographie, 1971, p. 66-96.

JEST, C. : Tarap, Une Vallée dans L'Himalaya, Paris 1974

JEST, C.: Dolpo, Communautes de Langue Tibetaine du Népal, CNRS, Paris 1976.

KLEINERT, CH. : Haus-und Siedlungsformen im Nepal-Himalaya unter Berücksichtigung klimatischer Faktoren, Diss. Aachen 1973. Hochgebirgsforschung Vol. 4, München 1973.

TICHY, H. : Land der namenlosen Berge, Wien 1954.

TUCCI, G. : The Discovery of the Malla, London 1962.

SNELLGROVE, D. : Himalayan Pilgrimage, Oxford 1961.

SNELLGROVE, D. : Four Lamas of Dolpo, Oxford 1967.

Conditions for the Success of Import Substitution and Export Diversification as Development Strategies in Asia

Bruno Knall

The vast majority of developing countries, in their attempts to place their economies on a broad, firm basis have been driven in the first phase of industrialization to emphasize import substitution. However, it is exactly in Asia that some developing countries on the basis of their respective resource endowments have chosen the export-oriented route. The last years have also seen some countries that previously adopted policies of significant import substitution switch over to export diversification.

I.

The Diverse Patterns of Development Strategy

Taking the predominance of the chosen development strategy as criterion (i.e., import substitution or export diversification), one can distinguish between two real types.

Among the *export-oriented countries* we can count Thailand and Malaysia as well as the city and island States of Singapore and Hong Kong. Their common characteristic is to be found in the fact that their exports are the main motor of their growth. Some concomitant import substitution has taken place in these countries; however, only with inconsequential encouragement.

In the other group of countries (the Philippines, Taiwan, Pakistan, and India) the emphasis in the first phase of development has been concentrated on the *substitution of imports*. In these countries, additional export promotion measures were taken later in order to stimulate and diversify foreign market goods.

The difficulty with such stereotyping lies mainly in the fact that each individual case is *sui generis* and, therefore, any classification can at best show merely the most basic pilot tendencies of the development strategy. For example, there are import-substituting economies that have sizable export sectors (sometimes even as a result of a conscious policy) while, on the other hand, export-specializing economies have experienced the replacement of imports by domestic products. With these qualifying comments we can now make explicit the basic premise of this paper, namely that import substitution and export diversification are by no means mutually exclusive activities. On the contrary, they are rather complementary development strategies between which many interdependencies exist. On account of this interdepencence, extreme development strategy positions (such as, *only* import substitution or *only* export diversification, completely neglecting the other strategy) can create structures that are damaging to long-range economic development. A proper "strategy mix" appears to be a much more reasonable (if not the only) approach to this problem. This mix should be determined by a variety of factors which are of an external and internal nature. *External* factors include existent or potential foreign markets, while *internal* factors depend much more on the domestic situation and on the prevailing domestic development strategy. These internal determining factors include the size of the domestic market, the resource endowment, foreign currency holdings, the level of industrialization, the intersectoral structure and efficiency of the economy, the general infrastructure with special consideration for the export infrastructure, the efficiency of the administration, and the educational level and learning capacity of the population, etc.

A. Countries with significant export promotion policies and relatively minor import substitution.

THAILAND

Until the middle of the 1950's, Thailand's exports consisted mainly of three products (rice, rubber, and tin). Rice, largely exported to Southeast Asian countries, made up more than half of Thailand's export earnings. In 1955, several liberalizing steps were taken that had an advantageous influence on exports. The system of multiple exchange rates, which dated from the end of the war, was replaced by a single rate of exchange. Export licences were eliminated except for rice, rubber, tin and corn. The export of sugar, whose domestic production cost was above the world market price, was subsidized. Finally, the government (partly with foreign aid) made investments in the rural infrastructure with the purpose of increasing the agricultural supply for both the domestic and foreign markets.

After a time lag, i. e., from 1958 onward, the results of the above measures began to appear in Thailand's foreign trade statistics. Agricultural crops like corn, tapioca and jute made up an increasing segment of the value of exports.

In spite of the export bias of the Thai economy, some spontaneous import substitution took place in the course of the economic development, especially in the consumption sector. In the industrialization process of Thailand the contribution of the Thai government was generally of an indirect nature, such as the provision of tax credits; the elimination of tariffs on important inputs by the Board of Investment under the authority of the Industrial Investment Act; low-cost loans which are made to medium-and large-sized firms through the Loans Office for Small Industries Development; the preparation of feasibility studies in selected industries, and the implementation of pilot projects designed to arouse the interest of the entrepreneurs. Since 1970 a new picture of import substitution has been visible in the Thai economy. Industrialization is still receiving official support, but according to a definite system of priorities. Those branches which use relatively labor intensive technologies and a large proportion of domestic raw materials enjoy the greatest encouragement. Nevertheless, despite noticeable (import-substituting) industrialization, Thailand is still a predominately export-oriented country.

In the development plan for 1972-1976 the need for export promotion is explicitly mentioned, and this was done in order to counteract an eventual tendency of the Thai exports to diminish over time. Slowly but surely import substitution is gaining increasing importance, even given that the State has avoided so far the establishment of high levels of protection. Surely there is no simple way in a liberalized economy to provide manufacturing industry sufficient protection so that not only import substitution will occur but also that a part of the output will be exported.

MALAYSIA

Malaysia is an export-oriented economy with liberal foreign trade practices in which private decisions have been dominant. Although she has concentrated on the export of a few primary products stemming out of her colonial heritage, she has benefited through comparative advantage. This specialization, of course, has been obtained at the expense of industrial development. Until now, the industrialization that has occured has done so without the protection of excessive tariffs or quantitative restrictions. Consequently, Malaysia today possesses industrial enterprises that are more efficient and competitive than in many other developing countries.

A special problem arises due to the fact that 44% of the population of Malaysia are Malays and 35% are ethnic Chinese. If industrialization continues to proceed with a majority of Chinese Malaysians, this could have income distribution effects with accompanying social and political tensions. Thus the case of Malaysia shows that the question "export promotion and/or import substitution" is not solely an economic problem. It must also be analyzed against the socio-political background.

SINGAPORE

With over 2.1 million inhabitants the economic structure of the island State of Singapore is comparable only to Hong Kong, particularly concerning the high degree of import dependence and the export orientation in connection with the industrialization policies. The specific character of the industrialization policy was (similar to Hong Kong) that although a certain import substitution was attempted it was mostly export-oriented from the beginning.

After the withdrawal from the Malaysian Federation in 1955, Singapore retained its import substitution policies as a means to industrialization; but because of the smaller domestic market the accent on export enhancement was sharpened. With the few exceptions of some consumer goods, the government avoided protecting the domestic industry through tariffs and quotas, in the belief that not only was the domestic market too small but also that the only way to establish an efficient industry was to allow the invigorating competition of foreign suppliers.

The reason for Singapore's rapid growth lies partly in the realistic industrialization policy, that consciously avoided sheltering the domestic industry behind high tariff walls. At the same time foreign firms were encouraged to build plants, and foreign capital was heartily welcomed. The fact that Singapore is an international finance center, and that she is the hub of the Asian dollar market, increases the attractiveness of this City-State for the foreign investor. Because of the small domestic market, she could not limit herself to import substitution, but was forced to systematically promote exports. Among other things, the economic expansion was supported by the availability of qualified, industrious laborers and a better than average public administration which conducted a healthy labor policy. Finally, it should be mentioned that there were some important exogenous factors at work, most noticeable of which was the Vietnam War, which strongly influenced the volume of foreign trade. A further factor was the unstable political situation in other Asian countries which led to capital flights; part of this money found its way to the Singapore finance center.

Of course, not all of the beneficial factors of the past will be at work in the future. The withdrawal of the United States from Vietnam (since 1969/70) meant a reduction in Singapore's exports. On the labor market bottlenecks have already appeared in certain areas. Nevertheless, Singapore has good economic prospects if the government continues with its previous pragmatic and innovative response to the economic challenges.

B. Countries moving from substantial import substitution to export promotion.

THE PHILIPPINES

The result of the import substitution policy during the fifties – effected through import controls and foreign exchange controls as well as tax exemptions – was a strong dependence of manufacturing industry on imported inputs because part of the new industrial output was produced by relatively capital intensive methods. Especially in the production of consumer goods, neither the possible backward linkages were properly considered nor was the resource-availability adequately examined. Furthermore, simpler goods demanded by the majority of the population received less attention than more sophisticated items, such as television sets, refrigerators, cars, etc.

If agriculture had been actively supported, the domestic market could have been expanded through the increase in productivity with the accompanying increase in rural income. Such a development of agricultural production, however, was not duly considered in the strategy which was dedicated to a one-sided import substitution. The other possibility of overcoming the limitations of the domestic market would have been the exports; but these lines of production received next to no help at all. On the contrary, they were sacrificed to the import substitution industries. Industrial production was sheltered from foreign competition by protectionist measures which allowed their production costs to soar; consequently, no appreciable export of manufactured goods could stand up to the world market competition. The increasing difficulty both at home and on the foreign markets led to a new development strategy after 1960. Import substitution was still a prime goal but export industries were given more encouragement. Thus, besides the devaluation of the Peso in 1962, which gave a welcomed impulse to the export sector, a whole series of export-promoting measures have been adopted. An assurance that in the future a definite policy of export promotion and diversification will be carried out is explictly stated in the Export Incentive Act of 1970. In the same year a stabilization programme was announced and a flexible exchange rate was introduced. The need for a new development strategy in the immediate future was very clearly presented in the revised Four Year Plan (1971/72–1974/75): the dependence on imports is expected to be gradually reduced and the supply of exports to be increased and diversified. This means, among other things, a re-structuring of the manufacturing sector, wherein it is hoped that a major contribution can be made to export diversification.

PAKISTAN[1]

Because of her low level of industrialization, Pakistan, immediately after independence, favored policies of import substitution. The turn to export promotion policies occured in a later phase of development. The early import substitution drive was determined by the fact that, before separation from India in 1947, the territory of Pakistan was almost totally devoted to agricultural production. The abnormally small degree of industrialization (measured by income, size, and resources of the country) can therefore be explained by the historical "division of labour" on the Indian subcontinent. The progress made in industrialization was quite impressive. The restrictive import policies and the overvalued rupee (the Pakistani Rupee had not been devalued along with the Indian Rupee in 1947) were the deciding factors for the import substituting nature of industrial growth.

This state of affairs began to change after 1955 when the country began to move over to export promotion. Of course, even before some of the exported manufactures were the products of plants which had begun as suppliers of import

(1) "Pakistan" in this context is taken to include East Pakistan (since 1972, Bangladesh), except where otherwise mentioned.

substitutes in the first half of the fifties (particularly in the case of jute and cotton textiles). But only thanks to the introduction of the Export Bonus Scheme in January 1959 could the exports substantially be increased and simultaneously diversified. Other export-promoting measures were income tax incentive for exporters, a credit guarantee system, and tariff rebates for various imported inputs of export industries. Besides traditional raw material exports (raw jute cotton, etc.,), increasingly intermediate and finished goods produced from, domestic raw materials were exported. Here Pakistan differs from countrie like Taiwan, Singapore, and Hong Kong whose industrial commodities are mostly produced from imported inputs.

As opposed to the first phase of import substitution – in which practically everything which was produced within the country met with domestic demand – the increased export activity has made the question of efficiency more pressing. On the basis of the domestic price structure and the favorable protective measures the industrial sector had developed at the expense of other areas. This disparity also had a regional aspect. The overvalued Rupee was a definite advantage for West Pakistan, where imports were much higher than exports. The reverse situation obtained in export-oriented East Pakistan. West Pakistan's balance-of-trade deficits could be covered by foreign exchange transfers from the East. The majority of industrial plants were built in the West so that a more rapid development occured here. These factors, accompanied by the unequal allocation of financial resources by the central government to the advantage of the West, should be counted among the causes of the hostilities which broke out at the end of 1971. Since 1972 Pakistan separated into (West–) Pakistan and Bangladesh. (West–) Pakistan had to follow a deliberate policy of substitution of imports and promotion of exports to overcome the serious economic problems. The develuation of the Rupee in May 1972 should be seen in this light. The result has been an increase of exports, but there is no doubt that more export promotion measures (such as marketing, quality control, export credit facilities, reduction of excise taxes) will be necessary in order to diversify the production structure.

INDIA

With the second largest population on earth, India has a (potentially) huge domestic market and comparatively little foreign trade (exports contribute only about 3 per cent to GNP). In spite of the fact that after the partition in 1947 India inherited almost the entire industrial capacity, industrialization was still on a relatively low plane. Consequently, the Industries Development and Regulation Act of 1951 and other legal and administrative measures (notably import quotas and tariffs) have given industrialization, by way of import substitution, a great impetus. The first important effort to promote exports, oddly enough named the Import Entitlement Scheme, was not introduced until 1957/58. However, exports increased only very slowly; the stagnating exports of processed jute can largely be blamed for this (next to tea, jute goods are the principal export items). It is probably a good guess that India's export promotion activities were too weak to prevent the introduction of Pakistani jute goods (especially after adoption of the Export Bonus Scheme) into the world market. A further cause for the low export growth rates could be found in the large number of partnership agreements between Indian firms and foreign investors, many of which demanded the price of curtailed exports in exchange for foreign capital and know-how.

With the devaluation of the Indian Rupee in June 1966, a step was taken in the direction of a free play of the market mechanism, but since 1970/71 a certain return to import controls is unmistakable. This development must be seen in connection with the government's goal of self-reliance.

Contrary to imports, exports exhibit a tendency to increase. The Export Policy Resolution (1970) makes it obvious that it is the opinion of the government that exports should be increased, with the help of appropriate measures. Since more than half of the export items are manufactured goods, an increase in exports potentially would depend on whether unused capacity could be better employed in the future. The existence in India of inefficient industries and much unused capacity shows the difficulties involved when one first attempts to establish an industrial base with the help of protectionist measures – in the absence of foreign competition – and then only later concerns oneself with efficiency. In this sense "growth" and "efficiency" are processes that should run simultaneously rather than successively. In India there is still a strong tendency to produce manufactured items for domestic consumption rather than for the world market because the home market offers a more certain assurance of sale and stiff quality controls and other additional provisions can be avoided. Even greater exertions and more effective export promoting measures will be required to realized the 7 per cent yearly growth rate of exports projected by the Fifth Development Plan (April 1974–March 1979). The Indian example clearly shows that industrialization should not be allowed to continue totally independently of the foreign sector (above all when it takes place in an atmosphere of import substitution). The most recent development points to an increasing coordination of foreign trace policies. This trend is an undoubted improvement over the former practice of supporting exports only when balance-of-payments problems appeared.

II.

Preconditions For a Successful Strategy of Import Substitution and Export Diversification

The sometimes discouraging experience with industrialization via import substitution (often praised as a panacea) has led in recent years to a reconsideration of the issues, and export diversification has acquired some support as the strategy best adapted to development. It would not be worthwhile to discuss whether or not import-substituting industrialization was absolutely necessary, because every economic development implies a certain diversification of the economy. A more relevant question is, however, whether the attempted import substitution has corresponded with the respective structures in each developing country. Therefore, the following presentation offers some normative success criteria, some oj which are based on observations made in Asia, others being introduced as plausible hypotheses.

A. Success conditions for Import substitution

At the outset, it should be emphasized that import substitution should not be confined to industrial production, but could also take place when foodstuffs or raw materials are import-substituted domestically.

Some of the difficulties that have arisen in the import substitution process can be attributed to the fact that developing countries have followed the model of of the industrialized countries, too closely, for example, by using capital intensive techniques, which has led to heavy dependence on imported inputs. Other obstacles have appeared as a result of inadequate protection, high costs, unused capacity, structural distortions, etc. Considerations like the above bring one to the conclusion that it is not necessarily import substitution as such but inappropriate (viz., inefficient and costly) import substitution that may cause difficulties.

The early phase of industrialization through import substitution should not aim at the erection of huge import barriers behind which the production of everything that is technically feasible, regardless of price, will be attempted in a mad rush for autarchy. It is much more realistic to concentrate on productive activities with a lower import component and in which the country has a comparative advantage or in which it will have the advantage in the foreseeable future. Furthermore, import-substituting consumer goods should be produced by using relatively simple ("appropriate") technology and priority should be given to goods which can cater to the needs of the masses. A most likely limitation on the choice of import-substituting products will be the availability of sufficiently qualified workers and entrepreneurs. Also, domestic raw materials and intermediate products should be used wherever possible.

A broad based policy of import substitution appears to be an appropriate program for a (large) developing country that has already reached a higher level of industrialization. For one thing, in such countries a certain familiarity with industrial processes has already been acquired. For another, a higher degree of industrialization implies a higher income with an accompanying enlarged domestic demand which would allow the realization of economies of scale. It is also likely that forward and backward linkages will play a role here, especially in the sense that broad productive activities tend to induce external economies. There is the danger, however, that during the process of import substitution the propensity to import of capital goods will rise, thus increasing the foreign exchange burden of the country.

As to the location of new enterprises it does not apear advisable to intensify the heavy and sometimes unhealthy concentration in big cities. By the same token, with the exception of small industries and handicrafts, the decentralization of plants should not proceed to the extreme point where every village has its own steel mill. A middle-of-the-road-approach would be a poly-concentrated industrialization located in *several* provincial centers surrounded by complementary agricultural districts. Another possibility is the creation of industrial estates that can be planned according to need and resource potential.

The earlier protected firms can stand up to foreign competition the greater is the inducement to economic efficiency and quality improvements. It should never be forgotten that protective measures in most cases can only be justified so long as the domestic producers are incapable of surviving exposure to foreign competition. These considerations imply that such measures should be temporary and their termination date should be fixed from the beginning.

This brings us to the different question of the form and intensity of protective measures. The object is to guarantee sufficient protection for new industries without creating cost structures which prevent their entry to world markets for a long time. Here we touch upon another success condition for an advanced phase of import substitution. Even though it may not initially be feasible to consider exportation of the newly produced goods, it is nevertheless advisable to remember that a time may come when this product could or should be exported (spillover effect). Even products which exhibit a high degree of price and income elasticity should, wherever possible, be produced in a competitive atmosphere with an eye to quality and price so that the transition from the domestic to the export market will be facilitated.

Among measures promoting import substitution, tariffs are frequently mentioned in connection with the infant industry argument. If the government of a developing country feels compelled to introduce tariffs it should strive for a uniform rate on consumer goods, intermediate products, and capital goods. At the least the effective rates of protection should not vary widely between branches of industry. It seems reasonable in the earliest stages of import substitution that the consumer goods sector should have more protection. But in a more mature stage of industrialization tariff discrimination can lead to misallocation and disproportionality in the production structure, thus thwarting the growth of intermediate and capital goods industries. In such a climate the complementarity required by economic specialization can hardly be realized. Also, tariff differences have unfavorable effects on the distribution of income.

Finally, it is important to remember that every tariff system that aims to promote the industrial sector necessarily discriminates against the agricultural sector. In many developing countries the essential role of agriculture has been too long forgotten. The vast majority of the population living in the country-side was simply overlooked, causing the requirements of an equitable income distribution to be left unfulfilled. The fact that higher incomes in rural areas would lead to a greater purchasing power and more consumer demand, was also not given proper attention. Furthermore, agriculture plays an important role as a supplier of raw materials for the consumer goods industry.

Protective tariffs are closely related to intra-regional trade. It would be to the advantage of everyone concerned if regional or sub-regional tariffs (especially on intermediate and finished commodities) could be reduced. The advantages of intra-regional cooperation could be exploited beyond the import sector to the entire foreign trade sphere and even to more basic considerations of production and investment. The possibilities for export opportunities seem quite good on the basis of experience with foreign trade between economies that are technologically compatible, because consumption patterns and quality expectations do not greatly differ. An intra-regional tariff reduction (possibly by means of tariff preferences) could, by excluding world competition, bring about increases in production and price reductions thus invigorating intraregional trade. A further possibility that would have to be investigated would be complementary intraregional specialization. The greatest stumbling block to regional cooperation is, of course, of a political nature. Nevertheless, should such a cooperation evolve in South and Southeast Asia, the problems of import substitution would still be relevant and merely extended to a much larger realm.

Subsidies and tax rebates are further measures that can be used to promote import substitution. The criteria for giving such incentives are of a very complex nature and in practice a reconciliation of individual measures is hardly to be found. Subsidies, provided they are on a sound financial footing, can do a great deal to correct maladjustments of the price meachanism and to promote the production of specific branches of industry (this applies to exports as well). A whole new field of endeavour exists here in relation to the unemployment problem in developing countries. Tax incentives and subsidies can be given on the basis of the number of jobs created, for the training of new skills, for experimentation with a new technology and many more purposes. These types of incenitves need not to be limited to domestic firms but can be extended to foreign based enterprises as well.

Quantitative import restrictions (often in the form of import licences) are a popular means of protecting domestic producers and at the same time keeping the volume of imports manageable with the available foreign exchange. Although there are a whole series of arguments favoring the adoption of quantitative restrictions of imports, experience in India and Pakistan, for example, has shown that these types of restrictions require a variety of complicated administrative manipulations (which cause enormous delays, among other things) and that it is extremely difficult to derive a system of priorities for such policies. The end result is frequently misallocation, inefficient firms, and unused capacity. Any government should, therefore, consider the possibility of replacing quantitative import restrictions with tariffs or excise taxes both of which (contrary to quantitative restrictions) provide additional revenues.

A system of multiple exchange rates definitely is preferable to a single but over-valued rate requiring tariffs and quotas for its continuation. Unfortunately, the more exchange rates are introduced, the more difficult the administrative problems become. Devaluation is the simplest means of achieving balance of-payments equilibrium. Experience in Southeast Asia has shown, that, where domestic prices climb faster than world market prices, several small devaluations are preferable to one large one. Relatively better results are otained when a devaluation is combined with other measures (e.g., import liberalization, stabilization programs, etc.), into a "policy package."

B. Success conditions for export diversification

Industrialization via import substitution is a necessary but by no means sufficient condition for steady economic growth in a developing country. With the passage of time, the possibilities for promulgating an inward-looking, i.e., a domestic market-oriented strategy disappear. As diversification of the economic structure proceeds, the export capability becomes stronger. Because of the increases in output the need for imports becomes greater. This in turn means a need for more foreign exchange. Thus the necessity to export must be matched by the capability to export. In general, export diversification must be preceded by a diversification of the economy which can be achieved best through import substitution.

In the "normal" chain of events the export of manufactured commodities is preceded by a phase in which the needs of the domestic market are first met, in other words the possibility for exportation develops out of production for the domestic market. The pre-condition here is that the export product must have a suitable price and/or quality to make it competitive on the world market. This so-called "spillover" is, however, not the ony conceivable pattern. It is quite imaginable that in some developing countries for very specific products the process could be inverted: Products that were originally produced for export could later be absorbed in larger quantities by a growing domestic demand. This possibility of "backward spillover", in which the foreign demand is partly replaced by the domestic, could hold great importance for some export-oriented countries.

The transition for a primarily domestic-oriented economy to one with a diversified supply of exports could take place without a systematic, conscious policy of export promotion. Such a process would, of course, require a much longer time. Nevertheless, it is not possible to exhaust all of the potential for growth without a closely integrated program of export promotion with industrialization policies via import substitution.

Via systematic export promotion it must be assured, in the first place, that the production of exportables is increased. On the one hand, this applies to the traditional exports (mainly raw materials) and on the other hand (and in particular!) to manufactured commodities. In the both cases emphasis should be gradually shifted to the production of those goods that show a long-run tendency to enjoy a growing world demand. This does not mean, that the developing countries of Asia should neglect in future the exportation of primary goods for some of which they are the principal source of supply. They dare not forget, however, that some raw materials face an inelastic world demand. Nevertheless, even in this area, all avenues may not have been exhausted. In the long run it appears to be in the interest of the Third World countries, in the light of the rapidly growing world demand for intermediate and finished goods, to first concentrate on the further processing of raw materials and to export more sophisticated products later. In view of their relatively better endowment with raw materials and unskilled labor (compared to skilled labour and physical capital) the developing countries should try to better exploit their location and cost advantages than they have done in the past. This implies the production of raw materials and labor-intensive outputs, where "labor-intensive" indicates that an appropriate technology should be adopted. The more industrialized of these countries have a greater comparative advantage in the exportation of manufactured goods than poorer countries because the number of suppliers of labor-intensive commodities increases rapidly and consequently the competition becomes keener. This problem is of great importance and decision-makers, indeed, should be aware that the present pattern of comparative advantage could completely change in the long run.

Still another requirement is associated with the transition from primarily import-substituting industrialization to export diversification. It is never too early to concentrate on high quality and low costs with an eye to the ability to compete on the foreign markets. There are many examples of the disadvantages involved in carrying out industrialization behind high protective walls and then only later attempting to compensate for the damage this does to the export position. As a rule such a process leads to inefficient methods of production, high costs, and quite frequently to unused capactity. Without the aid of appropriate measures from the beginning it becomes increasingly difficult to overcome the vested interest and the attitudes of producers which have appeared in the virtually risk-free phase of "easy" import substitution. In the development process "growth" and "efficiency" must occur simultaneously and not successively. Therefore, the healthy conditions of foreign competition must be introduced as early as possible in order to retain rationality in domestic production.

Among the most important requirements for increasing and diversifying exports is the availability of a suitable export infrastructure. The needs of export enterprises (well-organized harbors, credit, insurance, foreign market research, quality controls, export promotion councils, etc.) must be provided for, along with more sophisticated services that may be required for the newer manufactured exports. The ability of a developing country to market its goods abroad should also be considered as part of the export infrastructure. The developing countries should seize upon every opportunity to drive hard bargains with national and international firms in order to realize the advantages of the market position.

Inflation is also a problem which threatens the existence of a viable export sector. A tendency to inflation raises cost which pushes up prices rendering domestic firms unable to compete abroad. This problem has not received as much attention as more direct measures of promoting exports.

The measures for directly promoting exports also include subsidies, tax rebates, exports premiums, price concession on raw materials, tariff-free imports for raw materials, etc. The tying of subsidies to the labor factor (already mentioned in connection with the discussion on import substitution), is an interesting possibility which, contrary to the other measures, has seen very little practical application. All of these incentives stimulate exports but they also put a great financial burden on the State, not to mention the administrative requirements. As more of these instruments are used, consistency between them and the other development policies becomes a most difficult task.

The instruments of economic policy discussed above, were introduced to show ways to promote exports. In particular, they provide means of compensating for the disadvantages caused by an over-valued currency with respect to exports. In this regard, exchange rate policy is extremely important. One possible corrective action would be the adoption of multiple exchange rates. An interesting application of multiple rates in combination with freely fluctuating rates is to be found in Pakistan's Export Bonus Scheme. Traditional raw material exports did not receive a bonus, only the new items (above all, finished goods) received the help of the government. It is also informative to note in some developing countries that devaluation was accompanied by elimination of the multiple rates which would make this system appear to be an alternative to devaluation. A general devaluation might only bring a temporary improvement in export activity because structures based on tariffs and other restrictions could survive to counterbalance the effects of the devaluation (as appears to be the case, in India). Furthermore, a devaluation would indeed be questionable in the case of raw material exports whose world demand exhibits a tendecncy to be price-inelastic. Of course, if foreign demand for raw materials were income-elastic, a devaluation would mean a higher volume of exports but this applies to only a limited number of primary goods (as in the obvious case of mineral oil). In cases where a single fixed exchange rate is chosen after devaluation, a great demand is placed on the administration to ensure, through proper fiscal policies and allocation controls, that an efficient economy is maintained. In some developing countries a system of gradually changing exchange rates has been termed freely fluctuating. This is true of Pakistan's Export Bonus Scheme as well as of the partially free currency markets in Indonesia, the Philippines, South Korea, and Taiwan. More experience must be gained (on other continents as well) before we can evaluate the controlled "crawling peg" as an adequate exchange rate strategy.

C. Conclusions

Import substitution and export promotion represent the two sides of the development policy coin. Just as it is difficult to see both sides of the coin at the same time, it is a problem of no small dimension to correlate these two strategies. The individual country examples discussed in this paper show the complexity of this problem. They further indicate the frustrations and contradictions that arise in the implementation of an appropriate strategy-mix.—All too often industrialization via import substitution is attempted "at any cost", only to result in expensive production processes, inefficient methods, and poor quality. These effects of a forced import substitution are often intensified by the accompanying neglect of agriculture. At the other extreme, policies oriented at excessive export promotion fail to diversify the domestic production structure. Between these two models there exists a whole series of combinations that can be deviced from the two strategies. Interestingly – and also indicative of the methodological uncertainty in this area – intertemporal comparisons within *individual* countries often show inconsistent application of such policies.

The current popularity of intensive export promotion and diversification is undoubtedly the result of the sobering experience that many developing countries have had with import substitution. It cannot be over-emphasized that forced export promotion – exactly like forced import substitution – can also lead to structure distortions that hinder those sectors of branches which do not export. The question, "import substitution *or* export promotion ?" presents, therefore, a false alternative for a developing economy. Although there is agreement that import substitution and export diversification are complementary rather than mutually exclusive and that both policies should be based on a long-term perspective, the more pragmatic and operational question of the appropriate combination of the two strategies has not yet been satisfactory answered. At all events, a precondition for success is to avoid by all means exaggerations when setting up these strategies. A practical answer would have to spell out how the determining factors (some of which were mentioned on page26) are to be combined and what should be their respective weights and interrelationships. At any rate, very complex analysis of the determining factors permits the proposition that the alternative "import substitution *or* export promotion" is too narrowly conceived. This problem should not be isolated from other aspects of development. The increasingly important phenomenon of unemployment deserves first consideration here and, indeed, in connection with the adoption of appropriate technologies for developing countries. Furthermore, the role of foreign investment and aid must be analysed in regard to the political context of dependence and neo-colonial relationships. Finally, a whole group of social and political problems must also be dealt with in this analysis. When one reflects on the multiplicity and complexity of the contributing factors it becomes (alarmingly) clear that this "global strategy" is an interdisciplinary proposition that rightfully belongs to the field of integrated development planning.

The Iconography of the Buddhist Wood-carvings in a Newar Monastery in Kathmandu (Chuṣya-Bāhā)

Karel Rijk van Kooij

The wood-carvings of the Nepalese pagodas and monasteries are rightly admired because of the artistic skill with which many of them have been made. References to these wood-carvings can be found in several books on Nepalese art.[1] They were more in particular discussed in a monograph on Nepalese woodwork,[2] but not from the iconographical point of view.

In an article on the shrines and temples of Nepal, D. SNELLGROVE[3] has drawn attention to the many representations of Buddhist deities carved in the wooden parts of temples and monasteries. As his article is a kind of survey of the material side of Newar culture, he could not make a more deeply going investigation of the iconographical aspects. He did, however, mention the most important monasteries where Buddhist wood-carvings can be found.[4] An iconographical study of the Buddhist deities represented in wood-carvings has some advantages over the better known stone sculptures, although these are older and sometimes more impressive. Unlike the sculptures in stone, the images in wood are for the most part still in their original places, and, more important, they are not isolated examples, but form complete series. This is due to the fact that building in wood and the art of wood-carving remained for a long time a living tradition. The wood-carvers constantly made new representations of the Buddhist deities on the beams and struts which had to be replaced, and they followed the same iconographical rules, as had been carried out by many generations before. By the very reason that the old iconographical pattern has been preserved, we are in a position to study iconography in its context, and not from isolated examples; and we may expect that the meaning of these images becomes much clearer to us, when they are studied as a whole.

In order to retain the original iconographical pattern, I would like to give a picture of the groups of deities which have been carved in the wooden parts of

I thank Mrs. Dr. R. KLOPPENBORG for taking most of the photographs used in this article and for her useful remarks. I further wish to thank the FOUNDATION FOR SCIENTIFIC RESEARCH OF THE TROPICAL REGIONS for giving a grant for a journey to Nepal, and also the PRINS BERNHARD FOUNDATION for giving a subsidy for a second stay in Nepal.

1. See e. g. P. PAL, The Arts of Nepal, part I, Sculpture, Leiden 1974, p. 133. A. RAY, Art of Nepal, New Delhi 1973, p. 43–46.
2. S. B. DEO, Glimpses of Nepal Woodwork, Journal of the Indian Society of Oriental Art. New Series III, Calcutta 1968–69.
3. D. SNELLGROVE, Shrines and Temples of Nepal, Arts Asiatiques 8 (1961), p. 3ff., p. 93ff. See also M.B. JOSEPH, The Viharas of the Kathmandu Valley, Oriental Art XVII (1971), p. 121 ff.
4. An inventory of all the monuments of Nepal has recently been published by the Government of Nepal : Kathmandu Valley, The Preservation of Physical Environment and Cultural Heritage. A Protective Inventory, Vienna 1975.

Fig. 1 *Entrance*

Fig. 2 *Courtyard*

one monastery only. This monastery[5] is the Chuṣya-bāhā (Sanskrit name: Guṇākaramahāvihāra) in Kathmandu. Guṇākara seems to have been a famous Buddhist monk who was very much devoted to Mañjuśrī[6], but whether his name has any connection with this monastery is not known. It is striking, however, that the original deity to whom the monastery was dedicated, has probably been Mañjuśrī Dharmadhātuvāgīśvara, as we shall see below[7]. The building itself seems to be not much older than the 14th century[8]. Parts of the monastery have been restored in course of time. The wooden struts which support the roofs, and on which most of the deities to be discussed are represented, are supposed to be of the 15th century. According to an inscription in the monastery itself, a renovation took place in the 17th century[9].

The ground-plan of the building is that of an ancient Buddhist *vihāra* on a provincial scale. The entrance is marked by two lions sculptured in stone on both sides of the low doorway (fig. 1), and leads to a small porch serving as a lodging (Newari: *phalacā*)[10]. Behind this the courtyard is situated, which is surrounded by buildings on the four sides (fig. 2). They were the former residences of the monks, but at present they serve as houses for the Buddhist families, since the monks have married in course of time, and have founded families in order to maintain themselves among the Hindus, who formed the majority in the country[11].

The side of the monastery which faces the entrance contains a shrine (fig. 3) with the image of the main deity. The position of the shrine is indicated by a pagoda-like structure on the roof.

The wood-carvings which form the object of this study have been made in the struts which support the overhanging roofs on the street-side and on the four inner sides of the building. There are twelve struts on the outside, and twenty-two in the courtyard. There are, moreover, three tympanons (*toraṇa*), which are also provided with representations of Buddhist deities. One is placed over the entrance to the monastery itself, another over the door to the shrine, and the third is a smaller one placed over a side-entrance.

As D. SNELLGROVE[12] already pointed out, the identification of the deities

5. The word monastery is used throughout this article for the sake of convenience, although the Nepalese *bāhāls* are not inhabited by monks, but by Buddhist families.
6. Cf. Ch. B. SHRESTHA, Buddhist Geography of Ancient Nepal, The Fourth World Buddhist Conference, Kathmandu, Nepal, p. 5.
7. See p. 80
8. S. B. DEO, *op. cit.*, p. 10.
9. See A Protective Inventory........, vol. 2, p. 15.
10. Cf. M. S. SLUSSER and GAUTAMAVAJRA VAJRACARYA, Two Medieval Nepalese Buildings, an Architectural and Cultural Study, Artibus Asiae, XXXVI (1974), p. 169 ff.
11. See D. SNELLGROVE, Buddhist Himalaya, Oxford 1957, p. 108ff.
12. D. SNELLGROVE, Shrines and Temples of Nepal, Arts Asiatiques 8 (1961), p. 110.

Fig. 3 *Entrance to the shrine*

on the struts is in this case not very difficult, owing to the fact that the name of each deity is given in an inscription underneath the figure. These wood-carvings therefore offer a nearly ideal opportunity to study Buddhist iconography. The reason why these names have been inscribed appears from the way they have been written, and from the grammatical forms that are used.

The names are so clearly and beautifully written (fig. 37) that it seems unlikely that they have been meant for the wood-carver in order to make sure that the right figures were carved in the right place. They must have been intended for those who wanted to worship the deities denoted by them, whether these worshippers could read or not. In the latter case the inscriptions could have been explained to them by others, e. g. by someone belonging to the monastery. But the grammatical forms of the names seem to suggest that there is another, more important, reason for the presence of the inscriptions on the struts. Not in the Chuṣyabāhā, but in another monastery situated in Bhatgaon[13] the names of the deities have dative endings and are preceded by the syllable *oṃ,* e. g. "*oṃ lokanāthāya*", oṃ honour to Lokanātha (Avalokiteśvara). The inscription is meant here as a formula by which the god is invoked. In Buddhist (and Hindu) religion formulas or *mantras* are believed to be very powerful, whether they are pronounced, or written down on palm-leaf, birch-bark or paper, or worn as an amulet. The longer protective formulas, which are called *dhāraṇī,*[14] have been regarded as very effective against all kinds of dangers from early Buddhism onwards. The explanation of the inscriptions of the struts is probably that writing down the name or names of a deity is as much a means of invoking him as is his visual representation. The practice of giving the names of the deities right under their visual representation is a very ancient one, and brings us back to the Buddhist art of the first centuries B. C. in India. Some of the Yakṣas and Yakṣīs represented on the posts of the enclosure of the *stūpa* of Bharhut also have their names inscribed below, perhaps for the same reason.

In more respects the figures on the struts seem to continue the ancient Indian Yakṣas and Yakṣīs. Like their predecessors, the deities on the struts all stand in a particular posture, which is called *śālabhañjikā,* i. e. they stand with crossed legs under a tree, and grasp an overhanging branch with one raised arm. Although the term *śālabhañjikā* is generally explained as "a woman plucking flowers from the Sāl tree"[15], the architectural function of these figures, in India as well as in Nepal, is rather that of a caryatid. The parts of the building or structure upon which they are represented always have a supporting function, and their posture with one arm raised suggests that they have been conceived as figures which were to bear the part of the building on top of them. In a monastery called the Woku-bāhā (Sanskrit: Rudravarṇamahāvihāra) in Patan[16] the female deities carved in the struts stand upon a crouching dwarf-like being, in exactly the same way as the Yakṣīs of Mathurā.[16] Accordingly, the deities on the Nepalese struts might be regarded as the direct successors of the Yakṣas and Yakṣīs of ancient India. Only the names have changed, and additional attributes have been put in their hands in order to determine their identity.

13. This is the Caturvarṇavihāra.
14. Cf. L. A. WADDELL, The "Dhāraṇī" Cult in Buddhism, its origin, deified Literature and Images. Ostasiatische Zeitschrift I (1912–1913) p. 155 ff. J. W. HAUER, Die Dhāraṇī im nördlichen Buddhismus, Beiträge zur indischen Sprachwissenschaft und Religionsgeschichte, Stuttgart 1927. Fr. BERNHARD, Zur Entstehung einer Dhāraṇī, Zeitschrift der Deutschen Morgenländischen Gesellschaft, 117 (1967), p. 148 ff.
15. Cf. J. Ph. VOGEL, The Woman and Tree or *śālabhañjikā* in Indian Literature and Art, Acta Orientalia VII (1929), p. 201ff. See also: G. ROTH, The Woman and Tree Motif, *śālabhañjikā-ḍālamālikā* in Prakrit and Sanskrit Texts with special reference to the Śilpaśāstras including notes on Dohada, Journal of the Asiatic Society, Letters and Science XXIII, 1 (1975), p. 92ff.
16. Cf. P. PAL, *op. cit.* p. 133.

The general characteristics of the iconography of the tympanons (fig. 38) (*toraṇa*) continue an Indian tradition of a much later time. They have the form of a hemi-cycle, or sometimes nearly a triangle, and are crowned with a small parasol or have a small image on top. The border is adorned with a motif consisting of the head of a monster (*kīrtimukha*) together with serpents (*nāga*) and fabulous animals (*makara*). The monstruous head is often a lion's head with two arms, or in other examples a fabulous bird (*garuḍa*). It holds two serpents squirming down along the outer rim to the corners, where the two *makaras* with their curling trunks are represented. The whole motif is that of the *makara-toraṇa,* which is very well-known in Indian art. In particular in the sculptures of the Pāla period it was carried out in very much the same way on the rounded stelae against which the images were placed.

Within the area that is enclosed by this motif the main deity of the monastery is usually depicted[17] together with attendant figures forming his entourage. As Mañjuśrī is one of the most popular deities in Nepal, we very frequently find him represented in the centre of the *toraṇa* in one of his iconographical forms. Next to him we find Vajrasattva, Vairocana, Śākyamuni, Akṣobhya, Avalokiteśvara, Prajñāpāramitā, and others.

To a great extent the Buddhist pantheon of Nepal reflects the stage that Buddhism had reached in the Pāla period in north-eastern India. It is known that the great Buddhist centres of Nālanda and Vikramaśīla deeply influenced Nepal and Tibet. One of the monasteries in Kathmandu is even called Vikramaśīlavihāra (Newari: Thaṃ-bāhī), and the story of its foundation explicitly connects it with its Indian counterpart[18].

We shall see that many elements of the iconography of the deities represented on the struts and the tympanons can be explained with the help of iconographical works which belong to this period of the Pāla dynasty. These are the Niṣpannayogāvalī and the Sādhanamālā.[19] The existence of several manuscripts of these works in Newari script[20] from different periods indicate that they were actually

17. Compare the ancient Indian custom to depict the main god of the temple on the lintel over the doorway, e. g. the Śiva temple at Bhumara, the Viṣṇu temple at Deogarh, etc.
18. Cf. S. Lévi, Le Népal, vol. I, Paris 1905, p. 334.
19. Cf. Abhayākaragupta, Niṣpannayogāvalī, ed. by B. Bhattacharyya, Gaekwad's Oriental Series 109, Baroda 1972. Sādhanamālā, ed. by B. Bhattacharya, Gaekwad's Oriental Series 26, 41, Baroda 1968.
20. Cf. Haraprasad Sastri, A Catalogue of Palm-leaf and Selected Paper Manuscripts belonging to the Durbar Library, Nepal, Calcutta 1905, p. 34 no. 113 (MS. of the Niṣpannayogāvalī in Newari script). C. Bendall, Catalogue of the Buddhist Sanskrit Manuscripts in the University Library of Cambridge, Cambridge 1883, p. 40, Add. 1279 (MS. of the Niṣpannayogāvalī dated N. S. 995– A. D. 1875); p. 132, Add. 1593 (MS. of the Sādhanamālā dated N. S. 939=1819); p. 174, Add. 1686 (MS. of the Sādhanamālā dated N. S. 287–A. D. 1167).

used by successive generations of Buddhists in Nepal. Next to them the Dhāraṇīsaṃgrahas[21] should be mentioned. Although they contain very few iconographical descriptions, these works are nevertheless extremely important for our study of the deities of the wood-carvings, because the arrangement of these images will prove to be determined by the order of the formulas contained in these works. These formulas consist of the names of a particular deity and a series of sounds (*bīja*) without any definite meaning. They are used for the worship of practically all the gods of the Buddhist pantheon. The order in which these formulas are given corresponds to the order in which the groups of deities on the struts have been placed, as we shall see below[22]. If this is true, something can be said about the function of these images, viz. that they represent the Buddhist gods as Dhāraṇīs, which means that they are to be regarded as visual representations of protective formulas[23]. That they have been depicted in the same *śālabhañjikā* posture as the ancient Indian Yakṣas and Yakṣīs, who are equally protective deities, seems to underline that these images on the struts of the Buddhist monasteries represent divine powers with a protective function.

In the Chuṣya-bāhā, the monastery that is the main object of this study, there are two deities on each strut, a taller one standing upon a lotus flower or a mount (*vāhana*), and a smaller sitting figure, represented under the taller one. According to the inscriptions the standing figures represent the following groups: the ten Krodhas, flanked by Gaṇeśa and Mahākāla, the six so-called Cultgoddesses, the Pañcarakṣā, and a group of seven goddesses. The four standing figures on the side of the shrine do not have inscriptions but can be identified as the Buddhas of the four directions, on the basis of their iconographical features. Among the sitting figures we find the four Great Kings (Caturmahārāja), the group of twenty-seven Lunar Mansions (Nakṣatra) and three supernatural beings called Vidyādharas. After a more detailed discussion of the iconography of these figures, we will speak about the tympanons.

21. Dhāraṇīsaṃgrahas have not been published. MSS are mentioned in C. Bendall, *op. cit.*; R. L. Mitra, The Sanskrit Buddhist Literature of Nepal, Calcutta 1882. The present author is thankful to the director of the National Archives (former Durbar Library) for having the opportunity to consult the many MSS. of Dhāraṇīsaṃgrahas being in the possession of the National Archives in Kathmandu, Nepal. I also wish to thank the librarian of the Cambridge University Library for sending me microfilms of their MSS.

22. See p. 48. 60. 61.
23. Dhāraṇīs came to be personified in course of time, and were worshipped as deities. In Indian Buddhism only particular deities are deified Dhāraṇīs, e. g. the Pañcarakṣā, Prajñāpāramitā, Uṣṇīṣavijaya, and others. In Nepal the Dhāraṇī-idea seems to have been extended over the whole Buddhist pantheon. The Dhāraṇīsaṃgrahas start with the formulas of the five Buddhas (Vairocanadhāraṇī, etc.) and continue with the sixteen Bodhisattvas, the Four Great Kings, etc.

Fig. 4 *Gaṇapati*

Fig. 5 *Uṣṇīṣacakravartin*

Fig. 6 *Yamāntaka*

The roof of the street-side is supported by a row of twelve struts, six on both sides of the entrance. The names given in the inscriptions underneath the figures are from left to right: Gaṇeśa, Uṣṇīṣacakravartin, Yamāntaka, Prajñāntaka, Padmāntaka, Vighnāntaka, Ṭakkirāja, Nīladaṇḍa, Mahābala, Kekara, Sumbharāja and Mahākāla. Apart from the first and last mentioned, this group is known as the ten Krodhas, which are terrifying deities believed to protect the outside of a sacred area[24]. In the names of the inscriptions only Kekara is remarkable. This is mostly an epithet of Acala, indicating that he is squint-eyed.

24. M-Th. de Mallmann, Étude Iconographique sur Mañjuśrī, Publications de l'École Francaise d'Extrême-Orient, vol. LV, Paris 1964, p. 111ff.

Fig. 7 Mahābala

Fig. 8 Kekara

As a second name of Acala, Kekara also occurs in the Sādhanamālā.[25]

The figures have the usual demoniacal features belonging to terrifying deities, such as bulging eyes, a grinning mouth, a garland of severed heads and a brahmanical cord in the form of a serpent.

A crouching demon has been carved under their feet. All are represented in 'human' form, i. e. with one head and two arms, and they have a jewel in their left hands. In their right hands they hold the attributes characteristic for each of them, viz. in the order from left to right: disc, hammer with *vajra,* staff, lotus, *vajra,* elephants' goad, staff, trident, sword and again *vajra* respectively.

25. M-Th. de MALLMANN, *op. cit.* p. 129, note 11.

An iconographical description of the ten Krodhas in the first chapter of the Niṣpannayogāvalī[26] mentions forms with three heads and six arms, but in one of the left hands of each figure is a jewel, and one of the right hands carries the distinctive attribute, which is the same as that of the figures on the wood-carvings. The only difference is that Vighnāntaka has the double vajra (*viśvavajra*), and the staff of Prajñāntaka is marked with a *vajra,* according to the description in the Niṣpannayogāvalī. The main difference already mentioned is that in this text the Krodhas have three heads and six arms, whereas on the struts they have a human form, which is exceptional. The sculptures of the ten Krodhas hitherto known mostly possess 'non-human' forms, which is in accordance with most of the descriptions in the Niṣpannayogāvalī and the Sādhanamālā. A few cases of Krodhas in human form are known, but their attributes are different from the ones of the figures on the struts. It seems that the iconography of the ten Krodhas in these wood-carvings is but a simpler version of the tradition given in the first chapter of the Niṣpannayogāvalī. It is to be noticed that, apart from the four Buddhas, all the deities on the struts of the Chuṣya-bāhā have one head and two arms, also in cases where one expects more elaborate forms. The order in which the images have been arranged follows the Dhāraṇīsaṃgrahas, which give the formulas for their worship:
oṃ namaḥ daśakrodhāya// oṃ yamāntaka/ prajñāntaka/ padmāntaka/ vighnāntaka/ acala/ ṭakkirāja/ nīladaṇḍa/ mahābala/ uṣṇīṣacakra/ śumbharāja/ saparivāraṃ sapatnikebhyaḥ sarvvasattvānāñ ca sarvavighnavināyakānāṃ kāyavākcitta kiraya 2 vidhvaṃsaya 2 sarvamārān mārakāyikān yakṣān rākṣasān maho (ra) gān bhūtān piśācān devān manuṣān asurān kinnarān kumbhāṇḍebhyaḥ sarvaśatrūnāṃ hana 2 daha 2 paca 2 matha 2 vighnavināyanaṃ kuru 2 huṃ phaṭ svāhā // iti daśakrodhānāṃ dhāraṇī parisamāptaḥ//[27]
"Oṃ honour to the ten Krodhas//Oṃ Yamāntaka, etc., honour to their consorts together with their attendants; scatter (bis) destroy (bis) deeds, words and thoughts of all beings who put obstacles in the way; kill (bis) burn (bis) roast (bis) pulverize (bis) all Māras, beings that have the bodies of Māras, Yakṣas, Rākṣasas, Mahoragas, Bhūtas, Piśācas, gods, human beings, Asuras, Kinnaras, i. e. destroy (bis) the obstacles put in the way by them, and by the Kumbhāṇḍas and of all enemies, *huṃ phaṭ svāhā//* The formula of the ten Krodhas is now finished."
The language is far from grammatically correct, and for most people in Nepal the Sanskrit forms must have been mere sounds, which made the formulas all the more powerful.
The group of the Krodhas on the struts is flanked by the figures of Gaṇeśa and Mahākāla, who are often placed on both sides of a deity or a group of deities. They have the function of guardians, and their formulas also occur in the Dhāraṇīsaṁgrahas.[28] They are represented in 'human' form with their usual iconographical features.

26. Id. p. 111ff.
27. Text quoted from MS Add. 1326, Cambridge University Library, folio 150 b.
28. Id. folio 152 a.

Fif. 9 *Gītā*

Fig. 10 *Murujā*

Fig. 11 *Nṛtyā*

CULTGODDESSES (fig. 9–14)

On the struts to the left side of the courtyard, and on the first strut on the side containing the shrine six goddesses have been carved, named Gītā, Murujā, Nṛtyā, Vaṃśā, Mṛdaṅgā and Vīnā respectively. They are known from descriptions in the Sādhanamālā and the Niṣpannayogāvalī, and from representations in Tibetan pantheons, Javanese bronzes, and a painting of Tun Huang, but they do not occur very frequently[29]. The goddesses symbolize the acts that belong to the *pūjā*. They provide for the performance of music, singing and dancing as part of the cult. They are six in number, but in *maṇḍalas* they appear in groups of eight or four, and we find also others who represent the offering of a garland, flowers, incense, etc., and who are called *Mālyā*, *Puṣpā*, *Dhūpā*, respectively. Each goddess on the strut stands upon

29. M-Th. de MALLMANN, *op. cit.*, p. 162ff.

Fig. 12 *Vaṁśā*

Fig. 13 *Mṛdaṅgā*

Fig. 14 *Vīṇā*

a lotus under a tree, and wears a crown, a garland, and the usual ornaments. Gītā, who is the first of the series, plays the cymbals, Murujā holds the drum (equally called *murujā*), Nṛtyā displays the act of dancing and is pictured in the *ardhaparyaṅka* posture, whereas her arms make dance gestures, Vaṃśā holds a flute and Mṛdaṅgā plays another drum. The last is Vīṇā, who has a stringed instrument in her left hand, and plays it with a bow which she holds in her right. All of them have a placid appearance, and they represent the act of the cult which is indicated by the attributes they are holding, or, in the case of Nṛtyā, by her posture.

The four Buddhas (fig. 15–22)

The figures on the struts on both sides of the entrance to the shrine do not have their names inscribed under them. They have the same appearance as the other deities, i. e. they stand with crossed legs upon a lotus under a tree, and wear flower-garlands, crowns and ornaments. They are the only ones in 'non-human' form, i. e. they have eight arms and four heads, three of which are visible. They can be recognized as the four Buddhas because of their attributes and their mounts (*vāhana*). From left to right we find consecutively Ratnasambhava, Akṣobhya, Amoghasiddhi and Amitābha.

Fig. 15 *Ratnasambhava*

Fig. 17 *Akṣobhya*

Fig. 16 *Ratnasambhava, detail*

Ratnasambhava has two horses under his feet, and holds the following attributes:[30] (missing), sword, arrow, elephants' goad, noose, bow, bell (*ghaṇṭā*), and banner with a jewel on top (*cintāmaṇidhvaja*). Two elephants are visible under the feet of Akṣobhya, who holds: sword, *vajra,* arrow, elephants' goad, noose, bow (damaged), bell and a gesture called *tarjanīmudrā*. Amoghasiddhi has the same attributes in the same order, and is only distinguished from Akṣobhya by two small *garuḍas* at his feet. Amitābha, who is recognizable by the two peacocks serving as his mount (*vāhana*), holds *vajra,* arrow (damaged), sword (almost missing except for the hilt), elephants' goad, bell, (missing), bow (damaged) and a further lost attribute which should be a lotus.

30. The attributes are enumerated in the *pradakṣiṇa* order, i. e. beginning with the one in the lowermost right hand and ending with the attribute in the lowermost left hand.

Fig. 18 Akṣobhya, detail

Although some of the attributes are damaged or even lost, it is possible to recognize the scheme that has been followed. This corresponds to the description of the four Buddhas in the twenty-first chapter of the Niṣpannayogāvalī in which Mañjuśrī Dharmadhātuvāgīśvara is mentioned as the central deity of the *maṇḍala*[31]. Accordingly, we expected this Bodhisattva on the *toraṇa* in the role of the central Buddha. This is the case in the neighbouring Muṣya-bāhā (Sanskrit: Karuṇāpurīmahāvihāra), where the four Buddhas carved on the struts on both sides of the *toraṇa* occur in the same iconographical forms. As we shall see below[32], the central deity on the *toraṇa* of the Chuṣya-bāhā is Vajrasattva, who, however, has special connections with Mañjuśrī.

When we try to understand the "language" of this arrangement of attributes, we find that the four Buddhas have five attributes in common with Mañjuśrī: sword, *vajra*, bell (*ghanta*), arrow and bow. In particular the raised sword is a distinc-

31. See also M-Th. de MALLMANN, *op. cit.*, p. 102ff.
32. See p.75

Fig. 19 *Amoghasiddhi*

Fig. 21 *Amitābha*

tive sign of Mañjuśrī. The attribute in the foremost left hand of each of the Buddhas is his characteristic symbol: the banner with a jewel (*cintāmaṇi*) belongs to Ratnasambhava, the lotus is Amitābha's symbol, and the *tarjanīmudrā* is used as the specific gesture of Akṣobhya and Amoghasiddhi.

Through these iconographical means the idea is expressed that Mañjuśrī, who acts as the central figure, extends himself into the four directions, in each case retaining most of his attributes, but at the same time assuming the form of each of the Buddhas of the four directions by holding the characteristic attribute of each Buddha. Or one may say that the four Buddhas figure as manifestations

Fig. 20 *Amoghasiddhi, detail*

of the central Buddha, or that they are the Buddha himself in different aspects[33].

Since representations of the four Buddhas according to the iconography of the twenty-first chapter of the Niṣpannayogāvalī are not known from elsewhere[34], these Nepalese wood-carvings seem to be quite unique. The formulas with which the Buddhas are worshipped occur in special works with the title of Pañcabuddhadhāraṇī, but they are also inserted in the larger collections[35]. The text is very badly transmitted in the manuscripts, but it contains not much more than the name in dative ending, a few sounds and a protective formula. The fact that the Buddhas can be invoked like the other Dhāraṇī deities to give protection may have facilitated that the Newars consider the figures represented

33. Compare the remarks of D. SNELLGROVE in Buddhist Himalaya, Oxford 1957, p. 58ff. about the conception of Buddhahood as represented by the five Buddhas.
34. Cp. M-Th. de MALLMANN, *op. cit.*, p.110.
35. Cp. Ms 4–346, National Archives Kathmandu (Pañcabuddhadhāraṇī) and Ms Add 1326 folio 2 b, Cambridge University Library (Dhāraṇī-saṃgraha).

Fig. 22 Amitābha, detail

on the struts on both sides of the shrine as the Pañcarakṣā, the five protective goddesses, who are extremely popular in Nepal. In most of the monasteries these images are representations of the Buddhas, but there are cases that the Pañcarakṣā actually appear instead of the Buddhas. In a monastery in Kathmandu which is called Itum̩-bāhā (Sanskrit: Keśacandramahāvihāra) we came across six wooden images on the side of the shrine, only one of them being masculine, the remaining ones feminine[36]. The number of heads and arms, the colours, the mounts upon which they are standing, and their attributes, as far as they are left, correspond to the description of the Pañcarakṣā in the Sādhanamālā (no. 206) [37]. The one masculine deity can be recognized as Akṣobhya. (fig. 23, 24)

In the Chuṣya-bāhā the Pañcarakṣā have been represented separately on the next row of struts.

36. D. SNELLGROVE, Shrines and Temples of Nepal, Arts Asiatiques 8 (1961) p. 110 wrongly describes them as the six Buddhas.

37. We found the same iconography in the painted figures of the Pañcarakṣa in an illustrated Ms. no. 4–887, of the National Archives, Kathmandu.

Fig. 23 *Pratisarā, at Itum̧-bāhā*

Fig. 24 *Akṣobhya, at Itum̧-bāhā*

THE FIVE PROTECTIVE GODDESSES (PANCARAKSA) (fig. 25–29)

THE FIVE PROTECTIVE GODDESSES (PAÑCARAKṢĀ) (fig. 25–29)

The inscriptions, which appear again, mention the names of Pratisarā, Sāhasrapramardiṇī, Mantrāṇusaraṇī, Mahāmāyurī and Sītavatī. Those goddesses form the group of the Pañcarakṣā, who have come into being as personifications of particular formulas, and thus are original Dhāraṇīs. The oldest among them is Mahāmāyurī, whose formula already occurs in the Pali canon as a protection against snake-bites[38]. The four other goddesses are believed to avert the power of earthquakes, storms, wild animals, inauspicious signs, various diseases, etc. Representations of these goddesses in sculpture are known from the fifth century onwards, most of them in north-eastern India during the Pāla period[39]. Fur-

38. Cp. L. A. WADDELL, *op. cit.*, p. 163, 166.
39. Cp. N. K. BHATTASALI, Iconography of Buddhist and Brahmanical Sculptures in the Dacca Museum, Dacca 1929, p. 61 (Mahāpratisarā); D. C. BHATTACHARYYA, The Five Protective Goddesses of Buddhism, Aspects of Indian Art, ed. P. PAL, Leiden 1972, p. 85ff. and pl. XLVI. (Mahāmāyurī); L. A. WADDELL, *op. cit.*, p. 178.

Fig. 25 *Pratisarā* *Fig.* 26 *Sāhasrapramardiṇī* *Fig.* 27 *Mantrāṇusāriṇī*

thermore, there are numerous illustrations of this group in palm-leaf manuscripts. The examples hitherto known always have a 'non-human' form, i. e. more heads and many arms. The images in the Chuṣya-bāhā are worth mentioning because they appear in 'human' form. The attributes which they hold in their two hands correspond to the ones held in the two foremost hands of the 'non-human' forms: Pratisarā, who stands upon lions, has a wheel and a noose (*pāśa*); Sāhasrapramardiṇī holds a noose (*pāśa*) in the left hand and a *vajra* in the right. She has demoniacal features: a dancing posture called *ardha-paryaṅka,* bulging eyes and a garland of severed human heads. Two crouching demons are visible under her. The next is Mantrāṇusāraṇī, who has peacocks

40. Cf. D. C. BHATTACHARYYA, *op. cit.*, p. 85 ff.

Fig. 28 Mahāmāyurī

Fig. 29 Sītavatī

Left: Fig. 28a Mahāmāyurī, detail

for her mounts (*vāhana*), and forms the preaching gesture (*dharmacakramudrā*) with her hands. Mahāmāyurī holds a jar with three peacock-feathers, and stands upon elephants. The last is Sītavatī, characterized by two *garuḍas* carved under her feet, and forming the gesture of protection (*abhayamudrā*) with her right hand, and holding the noose (*pāśa*) in her left.

The formulas of the Pañcarakṣā can be found in the numerous Pañcarakṣā manuscripts,[40] and also in the large Dhāraṇīsaṃgrahas.

THE SEVEN GODDESSES (fig. 30–34)

A few manuscripts from the National Archives in Kathmandu[41] not only give the formulas of the Pancaraksa, but continue with another group of seven *dharanis.* This combination formed the solution of the next group of deities in the Chusya-baha, which consists of seven goddesses. In the inscriptions the following names appear: Vasudhara, Vajravidarani, Ganapati (sc. Ganapati-hrdaya), Usnisavijaya, Parnasabari, Marici and Grahamatrka. Individually most of them are sufficiently known from the Buddhist iconographical works, and from isolated sculptures and paintings[42], but as a group they at first seemed not to show any coherency at all. There is no iconographical work that mentions them as belonging together. Only the Dharanisamgrahas contain the formulas of this group of goddesses. There are even texts with the formulas of these deities only. They bear different titles, such as Vasudharadisaptadharani (The seven *dharanis* consisting of Vasudhara, etc.), or Grahamatrkadharani (after the last goddess Grahamatrka), or Saptavara (seven weekdays). Manuscripts with these formulas are mentioned in several catalogues, in particular the ones of the Asiatic Society and of Cambridge University Library[43]. They all contain the same seven dharanis always in the same order, and it is in this order that their visual representations in the form of goddesses appear on the struts on the right side, and part of the entrance-side of the Chusya-baha. We found a similar group in another monastery in Kathmandu, the Chun-baha. It seems that the wood-carver has followed a Dharani text as mentioned above, or perhaps a manuscript in which the Pancaraksa has been combined with the Saptavara. Like the Pancaraksa he depicted them with one head and two arms, and standing under a tree in the role of Yaksis. Several of the Saptavara manuscripts have illustrations of these goddesses, but represent them in 'non-human' forms. They also contain the formulas with which they are to be worshipped, the results that can be obtained for the worshipper, and sometimes an iconographical description.

41. E. g. Ms no. 5–299 and no. 4–887, National Archives, Kathmandu.
42. Cp. A. GETTY, The Gods of Northern Buddhism, Tokyo 1962, p. 130, 132, 134f.; N. K. BHATTASALI, *op. cit.*, p. 43, 58; B. BHATTACHARYYA, The Indian Buddhist Iconography, Calcutta 1968, p. 291, fig. 187, 188 (Vasudhārā); p. 277, fig. 156 (Uṣṇīṣavijaya); p. 285, fig. 173, p. 286, fig. 174 (Parṇaśabarī); p. 275, fig. 152, p. 276, fig. 153, 154 (Mārīcī).
43. Cf. C. BENDALL, *op. cit.* Add. 1315, 1356; R. L. MITRA, The Sanskrit Buddhist Literature of Nepal, Calcutta 1971 (reprint), p. 289f.; B. H. HODGSON, Essays on the Languages, Literature and Religion of Nepal and Tibet, Benares 1971 (reprint), p. 19, 39 (no. 144); Mss. no. 3–589, 5–299, 4–1598, 3–782 (582), National Archives, Kathmandu.

In one Nepalese manuscript[44] the name of Saptavāra becomes somewhat clearer, and it seems that this denomination has secundarily been attached to the group. Each time when the *dhāraṇī* of a new goddess begins, the copyist wrote in the margin the name of a planet together with the word *-vāra: ādityavāra, somavāra, aṅgāravāra, budhavāra, bṛhaspativāra, śukravāra, śanaiśvaravāra,* i. e. the day of the sun, the moon, Mars, Mercury, Jupiter, Venus and Saturn. It is perhaps possible that the title of Saptavāra originally denoted the worship of the seven planets on the seven days of the week, but was later on extended to the group of seven goddesses when the latter became associated with the planets. It is significant that the same manuscript has a painting of Sūrya (the sun) instead of Vasudhārā on the first page.

A parallel is presented by a work, called Pūjāvidhi, which is a priests' manual copied in 1573 A. D., and probably coming from Nepal[45]. In this Buddhist work the seven or eight Mātṛkās are connected with the planets: Vaiṣṇavī with the sun, Brahmāṇī with the moon, Maheśvarī with Mars, Kaumārī with Mercury, Vārāhī with Jupiter, Indrāṇī with Venus and Cāmuṇḍā with Saturn. It has been suggested that there "may have been a practice of associating the planets with the Mātṛkās"[46]. The whole group of seven goddesses called Saptavāra looks like a Buddhist counterpart of the Saptamātṛkā, which were originally Hindu goddesses, and it is probably on analogy of them that the seven Buddhist goddesses have been brought together into a group of seven in a period preceding the incorporation of the Hindu Saptamātṛkā into the Buddhist pantheon. The association of the seven Buddhist goddesses with the planets could have been caused by a similar process as with the Hindu seven Mātṛkās. The concept of Grahamātṛkā, the last of the Saptavāra, whose name means 'Mother of the planets' probably played a role in this process[47].

Four goddesses of the group are well-known from the Buddhist iconographical works, viz. Vasudhārā, Uṣṇīsavijaya, Parṇaśabarī and Mārīcī. Images of them are known to have existed from the Pāla period onwards[48]. But the forms of Vajravidāraṇī, Gaṇapatihṛdayā and Grahamātṛkā are not so well documented, and do not appear in sculpture; representations are only known from illustrated Nepalese manuscripts[49]. They have been found, however, by WADDELL in

44. Ms 4–1482, National Archives, Kathmandu.
45. Cf. P. PAL and D. C. BHATTACHARYYA, The Astral Divinities of Nepal, Benares 1969, p. 39f.
46. Id. p. 42f.
47. A description of the Navagrahamaṇḍala precedes the *dhāraṇī* of Grahamātṛkā.
48. See note 42.
49. A. GETTY, *op. cit.* pl. LXI (Grahamātṛkā); B. BHATTACHARYYA, *op. cit.*, fig. 229 (Gaṇapatihṛdayā), fig. 150 (Vajravidāraṇī), fig. 165 (Grahamātṛkā).

Fig. 30 *Vasudhārā*

Fig. 31 *Vajravidāraṇī*

some Tibetan Sādhana collections[50]. Accordingly, the wood-carvings of the Chuṣya-bāhā seem to be the first examples known in sculpture. We will now compare the group of the Chuṣya-bāhā with the illustrated Saptavāra manuscript mentioned above[51].

50. L. A. WADDELL, *op. cit.*, p. 190. WADDELL gives a photograph of a masculine "White Vajravidāraṇa" represented by a sculpture from Magadha belonging to the eighth or ninth century A. D. Its iconography is different from that of the Vajravidāraṇī of the wood-carvings and the illustrations in the Nepalese Mss.
51. See note 44.

The first goddess, Vasudhārā, is represented on the strut in 'human' form. The right hand holds a fruit, the left a jar (*Pūrṇakalaśa*). As Vasudhārā is associated with the richness of the earth, she is usually represented with a vase out of which ears of corn are growing up, or with a bundle of ears of corn. These are not visible on the image of the strut.

The illustration in the manuscript has a painting of Sūrya instead of Vasudhārā, as has been mentioned above[52]. Vajravidāraṇī is in the wood-carving represented with two arms. She holds a *vajra* in her right hand, and a noose (*pāśa*) in her raised left hand. The manuscript pictures a goddess in the *pratyālīḍha* posture, i. e. assuming the attitude of an archer; she has a red colour and a 'non-human' form with three visible faces and twenty arms. The next, Gaṇapatihṛdayā, has been carved on the first strut of the entrance-wall. The name in the inscription is shortened to Gaṇapati. It is a representation like that of a dancing Gaṇeśa, with a tray of sweetmeat in the left hand, and another attribute, which is not recognizable, in the right. Two rats are depicted under her, as her mounts (*vāhana*). The manuscript has an illustration of a 'non-human' form with one head and six arms. She also stands upon a rat in a dancing posture, and has a red colour. The attributes shown in her right hands are a kind of bag, an axe and a rosary. In her left hands are a fruit, a noose (*pāśa*) and an elephant's goad (*aṅkuśa*).

The strut next to the entrance shows a representation of Uṣṇīṣavijaya with a fruit and a jar as her attributes. This jar is supposed to be an *amṛtakalaśa*, i. e. a jar containing nectar, and has the same meaning as the spell used for worshipping this goddess, viz. a guarantee for a long life. Her 'non-human' form is found in the illustration of the manuscript, in which she has three heads and eight arms and the attributes usual for this form[53]. On the other side of the entrance we find Parṇaśabarī, who is provided with some demoniacal traits like a grinning laugh and a garland of severed human heads. She is furthermore distinguished by wearing an apron of leaves, which indicates her connection with tribal people, in particular the Śabaras[54]. These demoniacal features are also visible on the figure carved in the strut. She has one head and two arms. There are no attributes. In the manuscript Parṇaśabarī is substituted by Prajñāpāramitā, and the text is the Prājñāpāramitādhāraṇī. This substitution occurs in a few more manuscripts[55] of this group of seven goddesses. The examples of Parṇaśabarī in Indian sculpture show a somewhat different iconography.[56] There she has three faces and six arms, but the apron of leaves and

52. See p. 61
53. Instead of the second Buddha image, she can also hold an *amṛtakalaśa*, cf. A. Getty, op. cit., p. 135.
54. Cf. A. GRUNWEDEL, Mythologie du Buddhisme au Tibet et en Mongolie, Leipzig 1900, p. 152.
55. Cf. Ms no. 5–31, Dhāraṇīsaṃgraha, National Archives, Kathmandu.
56. Cf. N. K. BHATTASALI, *op. cit.*, pl. XXIII.

Fig. 32 *Gaṇapatihṛdayā* *Fig.* 34 *Parṇaśabarī*

Left: Fig. 33 *Uṣṇīṣavijayā*

some demoniacal traits are always present. The sixth goddess is Mārīcī, whose chariot is drawn by one instead of the usual seven pigs. She has one head and two arms, in which she holds a bow and an arrow. The painting in the manuscript has a form with three heads and six arms. Her main colour is yellow, but her right face is dark-blue and her left has the form of a pig and is also dark-blue. Her attributes are thread and needle, *vajra* and *aśoka* flower, and in her upper hands she holds arrow and bow[57]. This iconography is in accordance with her description in the Niṣpannayogāvalī, up to the blue jacket she is wearing.

57. Compare the images mentioned in note 42.

Fig. 35 *Mārīcī*

Fig. 36 *Grahamātṛkā*

The last goddess is Grahamātṛkā, the "Mother of the planets", who is again represented with one head and two arms. The hands form the preaching gesture (*dharmacakramudrā*), just like the main hands of the usually six-armed figure. In the illustration of the manuscript she has these three heads and six arms. Apart from the *dharmacakramudrā* she has in two other hands arrow and bow, and the upper hands hold a lotus and an attribute that looks like a bundle of flowers. Her colour is white, but her right face is yellow and her left is blue. It has to be noticed that the painting does not tally with the text in the same manuscript which mentions other attributes, viz. the *vyākhyānamudrā,* a lotus and a bunch of jewels (*ratnacchaṭā*), a spear and a noose (*pāśa*).

Grahamātṛkā is not only the last goddess of the Saptavāra group, but she concludes the whole series of figures carved in the upper parts of the struts. In particular this last group of seven goddesses, the Saptavāra, points to the fact that a Dhāraṇīsaṃgraha must have determined the choice of the deities represented in the monastery. We do not find this group of seven in the Sādhanamālā or the Niṣpannayogāvalī. There are Dhāraṇīs mentioned in these works. Vasudhārā, Uṣṇīṣavijaya, Mārīcī and Parṇaśabarī for instance occur in a group of twelve Dhāranī goddesses forming part of the *maṇḍala* of Dharmadhātuvāgīśvara Mañjuśrī. In this *maṇḍala* we also find the ten Krodhas, the eight Cultgoddesses, the four Buddhas in the same iconographical form as on the struts in the monastery, and the series of Lunar Mansions (*nakṣatra*), which is represented on the lower parts of the struts; but not the Pañcarakṣā nor the Saptavāra. Moreover, the total number of deities in this *maṇḍala,* viz. 216, by far exceeds the number of the struts. We can possibly say that some general ideas of the construction of a *maṇḍala* have been followed in the arrangement of the figures on the struts. Just like in a *maṇḍala,* the outside is protected by ten terrifying deities called Krodhas, and the centre is formed by the four Buddhas of the directions, the central Buddha being represented on the tympanon. Near the centre six Cultgoddesses have found a place instead of four or eight as are always found in a *maṇḍala*, and twelve Dhāraṇīs, who are not the same, however, as the ones mentioned in the Niṣpannayogāvalī. There seems to be no *maṇḍala* with the same deities as have been represented on the struts. These deities do occur in the Dhāranīsaṃgrahas and this explains why they have been carvéd in the wooden struts.

THE LUNAR MANSIONS (fig. 37)

Apart from the Four Great Kings (Caturmahārāja) who figure on the undermost parts of the four Buddha struts, and who do not show any particularities as to their iconography, we find on the lower parts of the remaining struts a series of twenty-seven Lunar Mansions (*nakṣatra*), represented in human form. They are present on the struts, because they too are believed to offer protection against possible dangers. All of them are sitting on various mounts or thrones in a posture called *sattvaparyaṅka.* They have the right hand in the gesture of giving boons (*varadamudrā*) and the left in a gesture of argumentation (*vitarkamudrā*). These hands moreover hold lotus stalks, the flowers of which have been represented at the height of the shoulders. The lotus-flowers indicate that the Lunar Mansions are associated with Candra (the moon), who has also two lotuses as his attributes, and who is called "Lord of the Lunar Mansions."

The representation of the Lunar Mansions is relatively rare in Buddhist art, and if they are depicted their iconography is not uniform. For instance the position of the hands may differ. The text of the twenty-first chapter of the Niṣpannayogāvalī, which is the only work that contains short iconographical descriptions of the *nakṣatras* according to the present knowledge, mentions the gesture of greeting (*añjalimudrā*). Another series of *nakṣatras,* which has been identified with some hesitation by P. PAL[58] and has been painted on a cloth (*paṭa*), shows that they have one hand against the breast, and the other resting on the thigh. The colours of these *nakṣatras* do not correspond to the ones mentioned in the Niṣpannayogāvalī. Only four of the twenty-eight are the same. In the Chuṣya-bāhā the colours have vanished, if they had been painted at all.

There seems to be more consistency in the mounts (*vāhana*) of the *nakṣatras*. Although these mounts are not mentioned in the Niṣpannayogāvalī, the ones of the *nakṣatras* in the Chuṣya-bāhā correspond to those painted on the

58. P. PAL, Two Buddhist Paintings from Nepal, Amsterdam 1967, p. 7.

Fig. 37a *Ardrā*

Fig. 37b *Aśleṣā*

paṭa. We see the following series: 1. Aśvinī - horse 2. Bharaṇī - corpse 3. Kṛttikā-throne 4. Rohiṇī - antelope 5. Mṛgaśirā - deer 6. Ārdrā - serpent 7. Punarvasu-*pūrṇaghaṭa* 8. Puṣyā - lotus 9. Āśleṣa - goose 10. Māgha - calf 11. Pūrvaphalgunī-mountainous landscape 12. Uttaraphalgunī - rocks 13. Hastā - elephant 14. Citrā-peacock 15. Svātī - throne 16. Viśākhā - goat or ram 17. Anurādhā - goose 18. Jyeṣṭhā - tortoise 19. Mūlā - root 20. Pūrvāṣādhā - cushion 21. Uttarāṣādhā-cushion 22. Śravaṇā - corpse 23. Dhaniṣṭhā - throne 24. Śatabhiṣā - calf 25. Pūrvabhadrā-padā-throne 26. Uttarabhadrapadā - throne 27. Revatī - landscape.

Fig. 37c *Pūrvaphalgu[nī]*

Fig. 37d *Hastā*

Fig. 37e *Citrā*

Fig. 37f *Svātī*

Apart from some minor exceptions[59] the mounts of the wood-carvings come so close to the ones on the *paṭa*[60] that both series probably go back to the same source, of which we have no knowledge. The question whether they reflect an ancient tradition or not is difficult to answer. We can only conclude that they are quite different from the ancient symbols for the *nakṣatras* mentioned in Hindu mythol-

59. Compare the list of *vāhanas* given by P. Pal, *op. cit.*, p. 33.

60. The close correspondance between the *vāhanas* of the Nakṣatras of the wood-carvings and the ones of the figures on the *paṭa* makes it unnecessary to hesitate about the identity of the latter. We can follow the suggestion of P. Pal that they represent the Nakṣatras. The *paṭa* belongs to the Museum for Asiatic Art in Amsterdam and represents a Candramaṇḍala. In the lower corners a story has been depicted, which Pal was not able to identify. There are three episodes, in which a certain animal plays the main part. The first scene on the right side of the cloth pictures a hermit, who accepts offerings from three animals, a monkey, a jackal and an otter. The last

Fig. 37g *Viśākhā*

Fig. 37h *Anurādhā*

ogy, in particular the tradition of the Purāṇas,[61] and also from the ones known to the Jains. It is likely that Buddhism had its own way of representing the

presents a fish. A fourth animal is sitting apart; it has apparently nothing to give. Trees are represented in order to indicate that the scene takes place in a wood. The second scene to the lower left side let us see the hermit again, who rescues an animal from the fire. The third episode is painted above the second. We see the animal taken by a god in a cloud, and brought to heaven. A sequence of events like this must indicate a famous Buddhist story, viz. the Śaśajātaka, the story of the hare, who has nothing to offer on the day of *uposatha* (the day of the full moon) and therefore presents itself as an offering by leaping into the fire. The ascetic, however, proves to be Indra, who rescues the hare and brings it to the moon, henceforth called *śaśin,* the one with the hare. The fourth animal, although clumsily painted, must be the hare who is the Bodhisattva. The story is quite appropriate in a painting with the moon as the main deity. For a discussion of the Śaśajātaka in the Ajaṇṭā paintings, see D. SCHLINGLOFF, Das Śaśajātaka, Wiener Zeitschrift für die Kunde Südasiens, XV (1971), p. 57ff.

61. Cf. W. KIRFEL, Die Kosmographie der Inder, Leipzig 1920, p. 138f. H. HAAS, Bilderatlas zur Religionsgeschichte, 12. Lieferung, Leipzig 1928. Die Religion der Jainas, p. 19.

Fig. 37i *Mūlā*

Fig. 37j *Śravaṇā*

nakṣatras. Some of the mounts have obviously been chosen because of the meaning of the name of the corresponding *nakṣatra:* Aśvinī (*aśva* - horse) has a horse; Rohiṇī (antelope) and Mṛgaśirā (head of a deer) are seated upon forms of deer; Hastā has an elephant because of its association with the trunk of an elephant (hasta); Citrā, meaning the variegated one, is seated on a peacock; Mūlā (root) has a root for her seat. Others are seated on lotuses, cushions, thrones or rocks, which may be an indication that no definite mount had been found for them. The choice of the mounts of the remaining ten *nakṣatras* is not so easy to define. In some cases the mounts might have been taken from the protective deity of the *nakṣatra*. Although we cannot be sure it is possible that the iconography of the Lunar Mansions in Buddhism does not represent an ancient tradition, because of the lack of uniformity as far as the position of the hands and the colours are concerned, and also because most of the mounts cannot be connected with any ancient tradition.

We will now leave the struts and discuss the iconography of the three tympanons (*toraṇa*).

Fig. 37k *Uttarabhadra*

PRAJÑĀPĀRAMITĀ (fig. 38)

The outer *toraṇa* of the Chuṣya-bāhā is provided with a representation of a goddess who is seated in a posture called *vajraparyaṅka* upon a lotus-flower. She has been adorned with garments and ornaments, and she wears a kind of *jaṭāmukuṭā*, i. e. her hair is tied up forming a kind of crown. She has one head and four arms, two of which form the gesture of preaching (*dharmacakramudrā*) whereas the upper right hand holds a rosary and the upper left a lotus with a

Fig. 38 *Prajñāpāramitā*

book on it. This is an iconographical form of Prajñāpāramitā, the goddess who represents the perfection of wisdom. As much of the material about this goddess has been collected by E. CONZE[62], we need not discuss her iconographical forms here.

More uncertainty exists about the attendant goddesses of Prajñāpāramitā. According to CONZE[63] they appear to be mostly Tārās. In that case the attendants on the tympanon are an exception to the rule. We see five goddesses, two of whom are seated in a relaxed posture called *lalitāsana,* and three in the lotus-posture (*vajraparyaṅka*). All of them are sitting on lotuses and are adorned with a crown and the usual ornaments and garments. They have two arms and hold a stalk of a lotus-flower in one of them. In the other hand they carry various symbols: a disk (of the moon) on a lotus in the raised left hand of the figure to the left of Prajñāpāramitā; a bundle of ears of corn in the left hand of the goddess represented above her; something that seems to be a flowery disk in the left hand of the one on the upper right side of the *toraṇa;* the goddess to the right of the central figure holds a white lotus; the small figure underneath Prajñāpāramitā holds the stalk of a lotus. This iconography corresponds to what has been prescribed in the Niṣpannayogāvalī[64] for the Pāramitās, viz. Ratna-, Dāna-, Śīla-, Kṣānti- and Vīryapāramitā. Groups of six or ten or twelve Pāramitās are represented in Buddhist art. The five attendant goddesses together with the central Prajñāpāramitā form such a group of six Pāramitās.

62. E. CONZE, The Iconography of the Prajñāpāramitā, Oriental Art II (1949), p. 47ff; III (1951), p. 104ff.
63. Idem, III (1951), p. 107.
64. Cf. M-Th. de MALLMANN, op. cit., p. 170f.

The usual six Pāramitās, which also appear in the Dhāraṇīsaṃgrahas, are *dāna-*, *śīla-*, *kṣanti-*, *vīrya-*, *dhyāna,-* and *prajñāpāramitā*. Our group starts with Ratnapāramitā and omits Dhyāna. Another irregularity is that these Pāramitās should have a jewel instead of a lotus-stalk in their hands.

The reason why Prajñāpāramitā is represented as the central deity on the tympanon is not only that this goddess is one of the most ancient and most famous Dhāraṇīs of Buddhism; she is also the consort of the main deity present on the *toraṇas* inside the monastery, once in 'human' form, and another time in a form with three heads and six arms.

VAJRASATTVA (fig. 39–41)

The Ādibuddha Vajrasattva occupies the central position on the tympanons of several Nepalese monasteries. In 'human' form he is depicted sitting on a lotus, his right hand holding the *vajra* before his breast, and his left hand, carrying the bell (*ghaṇṭā*), placed on his hip. He usually wears royal garments and ornaments.

The small *toraṇa* (fig. 39) placed over the side-entrance in the Chuṣya-bāhā presents this form. It is to be expected that the god on the main *toraṇa* (fig. 40–41) over

Fig. 39 *Vajrasattva*

Fig. 40 Toraṇa over the entrance to the shrine

the entrance to the shrine is also Vajrasattva. This is confirmed by the Newars[65] themselves. On the other hand the iconography of the four Buddhas represented on the struts on both sides of the *toraṇa* makes us expect to find Mañjuśrī Dharmadhātuvāgīśvara as the central deity, as we have seen above[66] Before we go into a discussion of the relationship between Mañjuśrī and Vajrasattva, which makes them actually interchangeable, we would like to describe the deity and his attendant figures on the *toraṇa* as accurately as possible.

In the centre a deity with three heads and six arms is represented. His colour must have been blue, as traces of the blue paint are still visible. He sits in the lotus-posture (*vajraparyaṅka*) on a throne in which two elephants have been carved. He has the royal garments and ornaments and wears a crown. His two main hands hold *vajra* and bell (*ghaṇṭā*) in the same way as Vajrasattva. The remaining right hands have disk (*cakra*) and lotus (*padma*), the left hands jewel and sword. Considering the blue colour, the position of the hands and their attributes, the elephants carved in the throne, and the 'human' Vajrasattva on the small *toraṇa* over the side-entrance, this deity is likely to be Vajrasattva. M-Th. de MALLMANN[67] mentions three varieties— all of them mentioned in the Niṣ-

65. Cf. A Protective Inventory, *op. cit.*,vol. 2, p. 15.
66. See p. 53
67. Cf. M-Th. de MALLMANN, Introduction à l'Iconographie du Tântrisme Bouddhique, Paris 1975, p. 420.

pannayogāvalī— of figures of Vajrasattva with three heads and six arms. The iconography of the figure on the *toraṇa* is in perfect accordance with the second form, which is described in the second chapter of the Niṣpannayogāvalī. The only difference is that the figure on the *toraṇa* has no female partner. Another problem is that the deity in the text mentioned is named Akṣobhya, but at the end of the chapter the same iconographical form is called Vajrasattva. M-Th. de MALLMANN is probably right in listing this deity as Vajrasattva, which is confirmed by Newar tradition.

The central Vajrasattva/Akṣobhya is surrounded by the four Buddhas : Vairocana sitting on a lion-throne on his right side; behind him Ratnasambhava on a throne with horses, Amitābha on a peacock to the left of the central figure, and behind him Amoghasiddhi on a throne with *garuḍas*. All of them have three heads and six arms. The two main hands of each figure are in the same position as the ones of Vajrasattva but hold different attributes: Vairocana has a disk in his right hand and a jewel in his left; the middle pair of hands carry a *vajra* (to the right) and a bell (*ghantā*, to the left); and the right upper hand holds a severed head, the left a sword. Instead of the severed head (*munda*), which is a very unusual attribute for Vairocana, we expect a white lotus in the upper right hand, which is called *puṇḍarīka* in the text of the Niṣpannayogāvalī. We wonder if we might consider this *muṇḍa* as a sort of "corruption" or a misreading of the wood-carver. Ratnasambhava seems to have his main right hand in the gesture of argumentation (*vitarkamudrā*) without any further attribute, but it is possible that the attribute has got lost. His main left hand holds a jewel. The middle pair of hands are provided with a *vajra* (to the right) and a bell (*ghaṇṭā*) to the left; in the upper right hand we see a disk and in the left a sword. Amitābha holds lotus (*padma*) and jewel in his main hands, *vajra* and bell (*ghaṇṭā*) in the next pair of hands, and dīsk (not distinctly recognizable) and sword in his two upper hands. Amoghasiddhi's main hands hold sword and bell (*ghantā*), his middle hands a double *vajra* (*viśvavajra*) and an unrecognizable attribute, his upper hands a *vajra* and a jewel.

Apart from a few deviations, which may be called 'variants' or even 'corruptions', the attributes of these Buddhas are in accordance with the text of the second chapter of the Niṣpannayogāvalī, where the four Buddhas surrounding the central Buddha are described[68], and it seems that this text has been the iconographical source of the wood-carver.

68. The text gives a slightly different system; the four Buddhas hold the same attributes as the main figure Vajrasattva, viz. *vajra* and bell, disk and jewel, lotus and sword; each Buddha has a lotus of a different colour, white, yellow, red and green respectively, according to the colour of that Buddha. On the *toraṇa*, the order of the attributes changes each time. See Niṣpannayogāvalī, edited by B. BHATTACHARYYA, Baroda 1972, second chapter (Piṇḍīkramoktākṣobhyamandalam).

Fig. 41 *Detail of the right side of fig.* 40 *fig.* 41a *Detail of the left side of Fig.* 40

As we have said above, one does not expect Vajrasattva as the central figure on the main *torana,* but rather a representation of Mañjuśrī Dharmadhātuvāgīśvara. There is, however, reason to suppose that both are so closely related that they sometimes become interchangeable. M-Th. de MALLMANN [69] has noticed some cases of assimilation between the two deities. In the twentieth chapter of the Niṣpannayogāvalī the central Buddha is called Mañjuvajra, "who has the nature of Vairocana" and "who is adorned with Vajrasattva, being his reflection (*svābhā*)". In the first chapter of the same work the central deity is Vajrasattva, "who has the form of Mañjuvajra". In Sādhanamālā 67, Vajrasattva takes the central position in a *maṇḍala* of Siddhaikavīra Mañjuśrī.

In a later article[70] De MALLMANN agrees with a remark made by A. BAREAU, that in tantric Buddhism a kind of unification had taken place between the transcendant Buddhas and certain great Bodhisattvas, in this case between Vajrasattva/Vairocana and Mañjuśrī.

69. M-Th. de MALLMANN, Étude Iconographique sur Mañjuśrī, Paris 1964, p. 103.
70. Idem, "Dieux Polyvalents" du Tantrisme Bouddhique, Journal Asiatique CCLII (1964), p. 365.

Fig. 41a *Detail of the left side of Fig-* 40

*Fig.*41*b Detail of the right side of fig.*40

The evidence of the Nepalese *toraṇas* seems to confirm this, and in order to show in what way the interrelationship between Vajrasattva and Mañjuśrī is expressed, we have to discuss a few *toraṇas* belonging to other monasteries in Kathmandu and Patan.

Mañjuśrī Dharmadhātuvāgīśvara

Following M-Th. de Mallmann[71] we only call one form of Mañjuśrī by this name, viz. when he has four heads and eight arms, forming the gesture of preaching (*dharmacakramudrā*) with his main hands, and holding *vajra* and bell (*ghaṇṭā*), arrow and bow, and sword and book in the second, third and upper pairs of hands respectively. He is seated on a lion-throne, he has a white colour and he is adorned with the royal garments and ornaments.

Fig. 42 *Tympanon with a representation of Mañjuśrī Dharmadhātuvāgīśvara, Tham-bahi, Kathmandu*

71. M-Th. de Mallmann, Étude Iconographique sur Mañjuśrī, Paris 1964, p. 61.

Fig. 43 *Tympanon at Biṃche-bāhā, Patan*

This iconographical form of Mañjuśrī can frequently be found on tympanons of Nepalese monasteries. In the Thaṃ-bāhī (Sanskrit : Vikramaśīlamahāvihāra) we see Mañjuśrī Dharmadhātuvāgīśvara (fig. 42) accompanied by Avalokiteśvara Ṣaḍakṣarī and Prajñāpāramitā, forming the triad Buddha (Mañjuśrī), Dharma (Prajñāpāramitā) and Saṅgha (Avalokiteśvara). The central Mañjuśrī is furthermore surrounded by the four Buddhas in 'human' form recognizable by their colours and gestures (*mudrās*). On the outer rim we see two more attendant deities, and on top is the image of Vajrasattva as Ādibuddha. He is represented in 'human' form holding the *vajra,* which is painted blue, in his right hand before his breast, and the bell (*ghaṇṭā*), painted yellow, in his left hand on his hip.

The same pattern is found on the tympanon of the Bhiṃche-baha (Sanskrit: Mayūravarṇamahāvihāra) in Patan, where even the syllable *aḥ,* which is the particular sound (*bīja*) of Mañjuśrī Dharmadhātuvāgīśvara, has been painted on the cloth hanging down from his throne. Here we also see Vajrasattva sitting on top of the *toraṇa* (fig. 43).

A representation of Vajrasattva in 'non-human' form, likewise on top of a *toraṇa*, with Mañjuśrī Dharmadhātuvāgīśvara as the central deity, can be found in the Haka-bāhā (Sanskrit: Ratnākaramahāvihāra) in Patan. He has four heads and eight arms. The first pair of arms is held in the position which is characteristic for Vajrasattva, and carry *vajra* and bell (*ghaṇṭā*). The raised sword, which is the distinctive symbol of Mañjuśrī, is in his upper right hand. The other attributes are difficult to recognize because of the damaged condition of the *toraṇa*.

This 'non-human' form of Vajrasattva, which is not known from elsewhere, seems to have been influenced by the iconographical form of the central Mañjuśrī Dharmadhātuvāgīśvara, from whom he has taken over the four heads and the eight arms and the raised sword in his upper right hand. In the same way the iconography of the four Buddhas of the directions, when they are represented with four heads and eight arms, has been assimilated to that of the central figure of Mañjuśrī, as we have seen. Better than calling this "a kind of unification between the transcendant Buddhas and certain great Bodhisattvas", it is to bear in mind that Mañjuśrī Dharmadhātuvāgīśvara has not the function of a Bodhisattva in this iconographical context, but represents the central Buddha Vairocana and is called a Buddha himself. And as such he extends himself into the four directions as the four Buddhas, who can assume the same 'non-human' forms as the central Buddha, and into the uppermost direction as the Ādibuddha Vajrasattva, who too takes the appearance of the central 'Buddha'. In this way these iconographical assimilations express the idea that there is fundamentally one Buddha. Vajrasattva is, in this context, an aspect of the 'Buddha' Mañjuśrī Dharmadhātuvāgīśvara, and he takes the same iconographical form, with the only difference that the Vajrasattva aspect has a *vajra* in his first right hand, and a bell (*ghaṇṭā*) in his first left hand, whereas Mañjuśrī forms the *dharmacakra-mudrā* with his two main hands. On another *toraṇa* in the same Haka-bāhā we found that Vajrasattva in this form and Mañjuśrī had changed positions, the former appearing in the centre, and the latter on top. The two forms apparently became interchangeable. It is to be noticed that this Vajrasattva is accompanied by another form of Mañjuśrī called Mañjuvajra[72]. The interchangeability of Vajrasattva and Mañjuśrī Dharmadhātuvāgīśvara might be the reason why we find Vajrasattva as the central deity on the *toraṇa* of the Chuṣya-bāhā, and not the expected Mañjuśrī Dharmadhātuvāgīśvara. It remains still enigmatic why the Vajrasattva of the Chuṣya-bāhā has not the iconographical aspects of Mañjuśrī Dharmadhātuvāgīśvara like the ones mentioned above, but is iconographically related to Akṣobhya. The possibility has to be considered that this *toraṇa* has replaced an older one, which had the correct iconography.

72. The deity has three heads and six arms. The attributes and gestures are in *pradakṣiṇā : varadamudrā*, arrow, sword, blue lotus, bow and book. He sits in the lotus posture upon a lotus. This iconography corresponds to the description of Mañjuvajra in the Sādhanamālā (no. 76) and the Niṣpannayogāvalī (20th chapter).

On the other hand it is important to notice that Vajrasattva is frequently invoked at the very beginning of several Dhāraṇīsaṃgrahas. The Vajrasattva figure of the present *toraṇa* might have been chosen because of the many Dhāraṇīs depicted on the struts.

Concluding remarks

By studying the complete iconography of one sacred building, in this case of a Newar monastery in Kathmandu, it is possible to obtain a better understanding of the meaning of the series of images represented in the wood-carvings of the struts and the tympanons. The iconography of the Chuṣya-bāhā seems to have been determined by some Dhāraṇīsaṃgraha, at the beginning of which Vajrasattva is invoked. He is depicted on the main *toraṇa* over the entrance to the shrine. His consort is Prajñāpāramitā, who is represented on the outer *toraṇa* over the entrance to the monastery itself. Then follow the Dhāraṇīs of the four Buddhas, who are to be seen on the struts on both sides of the entrance to the shrine; after these we find the Pañcarakṣā and the Saptavāra, who are Dhāraṇī-goddesses *par excellence*, and on the struts on both sides of the outer entrance are the ten Krodhas flanked by Gaṇeśa and Mahākāla, whose formulas also appear in the Dhāraṇīsaṃgrahas. At last the Four Great Kings and the twenty-seven Nakṣatras have been represented on the lowermost parts of the struts, in the same role of protective deities.

Pronouncing their names, which have in most cases been inscribed under the visual representations of these deities, and presenting offerings is a means of protection against all kind of disasters like loss of health, damage caused by earthquakes, storms, drought, etc. Going about the sides of the residences around the courtyard, and worshipping the deities depicted on the struts supporting the roofs, must have had the same value as reading a Dhāraṇīsaṃgraha, viz. a kind of insurance against the vicissitudes of life.

We have also seen that the iconographical forms of the deities represented have been taken from works like the Sādhanamālā and the Niṣpannayogāvalī, sometimes in simplified versions. The images, however, have not been arranged in the form of a *maṇḍala,* in contrast to the system used in the Niṣpannayogāvalī. The Newar Buddhists are no tantric adepts who wanted to become one with the supreme deity. The deities on the wood-carvings are there for protection and in order to assure a reasonable measure of safety to the people living in this monastery.

Nepal in the Early Medieval Period: Gleanings from the Bendall Vaṁśāvali

Thakur Lal Manandhar

We have interesting glimpses of the state of the country and the condition of the people during the early mediaeval period of Nepalese history, thanks to the records kept in the Bendall *Vaṁśāvalī*[1]. The information derived from this source is supplemented by the testimony of contemporary inscriptions and colophons of Nepalese manuscripts.

In Nepal, since very early times monarchy has been the only form of Government which demanded serious attention. The divine character of Kingship was accepted, and it was in most cases, hereditary.

In the early mediaeval period, we find a few cases of nomination of a King by a preceding ruler and also by a very powerful noble of royal descent. An instance of popular election also is there which is exceptional in the case of the enthronement of King Jayarājadeva of the *Bhōta* royal descent in 1347 A.D. This was meant to restore the union of the two royal houses which had broken down earlier after the death of King Anantamalla in 1308 A.D.

A ruler who was nominated by his predecessor or by one in power is described as *Puṣyābhiṣekarāja*.[2]. According to Dharma Śāstra, *Puṣyābhiṣeka*[2] is a shorter rite of crowning a King in the Puṣya constellation, usually a year after the demise of his predecessor. This type of coronation had then become a tradition in Nepal, which is evidenced by the Bendall Vaṁśāvalī.

Early instances are those of Rudradeva (1167–1175 A.D.)[3], Someśvaradeva

1. Later named as *Gopālarāja Vaṁśāvalī,* now in the National Archives Ms. No. 1–1593 (Jtihāsa 6)
2. The SāmaVidhāna-Brāhmaṇa describes a shorter rite: "The priest should crown the king when the moon is in the Puṣya or Śrāvaṇa constellation".
   —History of Dharma Śāstra by
   P. V. Kane, vol. 3, p. 70.
3. *Saṃvat* 267 *Pauṣa-kṛṣṇa-trayodaśyāṃ śukra dine Śrī-Rudradeva puṣyābhiṣeka kṛtavān* (On Friday, the 13th day of the month of Pauṣa, dark fortnight, Śrī Rudradeva was crowned as *Puṣyābhiṣekarāja,* in the year 267 N. E.)

(1178–1182 A.D.)[4] and Guṇakāmadeva (1184–1196 A.D.)[5]. An information regarding the conditions or circumstances which led to their nomination is absent, but in the case of the later kings such as Jayabhīmadeva (1258–1271 A.D.), Jayasīhamaladeva (1271–1274 A.D.), Anantamaladeva (1274–1308 A.D.) and lastly Jayārimalladeva (1320–1344 A.D.), we get some clues in this Vaṁśāvalī[6].

A state of turmoil, which had started in the closing years of the reign of King Abhayamalla (1216–1255 A.D.), took a serious turn at the time of his successor King Jayadeva (1255–1258 A.D.). Two insurgents, namely Jayabhīmadeva of the *Bhõta*[7] royal house and Jayasīhamaladeva of *Tripura*[8] royal house, both made a compromise, as it seems, and unitedly forced King Jayadeva to abdicate in their favour. Probably they made an agreement, by virtue of which Jayabhīmadeva was crowned King as *Puṣyābhiṣekarāja* and Jayasīhamaladeva was nominated as his successor, and the latter, when he became king, was in turn to nominate Anantamalla as his successor. It seems as if a roll of succession was drawn, and according to seniority, the sons of those who were in the roll were to do likewise, since we find King Anantamalla, later in his turn, nominated Jayādityadeva, the son of King Jayabhīmadeva, as his successor. This looks exactly like the roll of succession drawn among the Rāṇas later, at the turn of this century.

4. *Saṃvat 299 Kārtika-kṛṣṇa-ṣaṣṭhi śukravāra*
rā (ja Śrī) Someśvaradeva puṣyābhiṣeka kṛtavān
(On Friday, the 6th day of the month of Kārtik, dark fortnight, Someśvaradeva was crowned as *Puṣyābhiṣekarāja* in the year 299 N. E.)
—The Kaiser fragment of "Vaṁśāvalī" in Medieval History of Nepal by L. Petech, appendix V, p. 215.
5. *rāja Śrī-Guṇakāmadeva Puṣyabhiṣeka kṛtya rājya varṣa* 3. (folio 25)
(King Śrī Guṇakāmadeva was crowned as *Puṣyābhiṣekarāja*. He ruled for 3 years)
6. *Puṣyābhiṣeka-rāja Śrī-Jayabhīmadeva varṣa* 13 *mā* 3.
Puṣyābhiṣeka-rāja Śrī-Jayasīhamaladeva varṣa 2 *mā* 7.
Puṣyābhiṣeka-rāja Śrī-Anantamaladeva varṣa 32 *mā* 10. (folio 25)
Śrī Jayarudramala, devasya prabhūtena svakuṭumba Śrī-Jayārimaladevasya puṣyābhiṣeka kṛtya, rājābhuktimātran dadau. (folio. 27)
Śrī Jayabhīmadeva was crowned as *Puṣyābhiṣeka-rāja.* He ruled for 13 years and 3 months.
Śrī Jayasīhamaladeva was crowned as *Puṣyābhiṣeka-rāja.* He ruled for 2 years and 7 months.
Śrī Anantamaladeva was crowned as *Puṣyābhiṣeka-rāja.* He ruled for 32 years 10 months.
Śrī Jayārimaladeva was crowned as *Puṣyābhiṣeka-rāja* by virtue of Śrī Jayarudramaladeva's power. He was related to the latter as his own kinsman. He was given only a nominal kingship')
—from the Sanskrit portion of the Bendall *Vaṁśāvalī*, fol. 25, 26 and 27.
7. *Bhõta,* now used in Newari for Banepā, was the eastern principality beyond Bhaktapur.
8. *Tripura* is used for Bhaktapur in this *Vaṁśāvalī.*

Also, this turned out to be practically a joint venture or partnership between the two royal houses, in as much as they used to share the income of the state. After the death of King Anantamalla, the state of *Bhõta*, e.g. the eastern principality had to forefeit its share of the income from the central authority[9] of *Gwãla*[10]. The original agreement supposedly made at the time of Jayabhīmadeva broke down.

In 1320 A.D. Jayārimalla, the son of King Anantamalla was crowned king in *Gwãla* (the modern Deo Patan) without being invested with full authority. It was his turn this time to be a *Puṣyābhiṣekarāja*, a king by nomination. It seems, that although he was only a figure head, the older tradition was respected in this case by Jayarudramalla of the *Tripura* royal house, who was then in power. In the mean time, Jayānandadeva was ruling as a sovereign in *Bhõta,* though not recognised then by the *Tripura* royal house. The relation between the two royal houses remained strained. It was only in 1347 A.D. that the re-union of the two royal houses was achieved by Devaladevī[11], the astute lady politician at the time working in the capacity of a powerful regent of the *Tripura* royal house, during the minority of her grand daughter Rājalladevī. Earlier, Paśupatimalla, probably the son of King Jayārimalla, had created trouble, by claiming the kingship as a rightful heir to the throne, but this was suppressed in no time and he was thrown into prison.

By common consent of the two royal houses, and by popular support of nobles, Devaladevī managed to enthrone Jayarājadeva in 1347 A.D.[12] In this case, he is not styled as *Puṣyābhiṣekarāja*, perhaps because he was the rightful heir to succeed his father Jayānandadeva, who was recognised as a sovereign King of Nepal. So it is obvious, that only the coronation ceremony of a king who

9. *Gwãla* is used to indicate the Central Authority in Deo Pāṭan.
10. *Sa* 427 *Śrāvaṇa sudi saptamī Śrī Anantamaladevasa......**Bhõta*** *waṅa dãchi liva abhāga juwa......thvana lisa Bhõta yā Gwãla āya ma thyākato* (folio 41). (N. E. 427 Śrāvaṇa, bright fortnight 7, King Anantamalla left Deo Pāṭan for *Bhõta* (Banepā); a year later he died. Since then the *Bhõta* (Banepā) kingdom was deprived of its share of the income by the *Gwãla* kingdom (Central authority of Nepal)
11. *Sa* 468 *Bhādrapada sudi* 13 *Śrī-Jayarājadevasa Gwãlasa ganṭha thācaka tõ. Śrī-Devaladevī......thva Kṣana lisa ni Bhõta yā Gwãla āya thyākva tõ.* (Jayarājadeva was proclaimed king in *Gwãla* (Deo Pāṭan) by Śrī Devaladevī. From that time onward the *Bhõta* (Banepā) kingdom regained its share of income from *Gwãla* kingdom (Central authority of Nepal (folio 51.) —Newari portion of the Bendall *Vaṁśāvalī.*
12. *Ubhaya-rāja-kula-Sānumatena saṃvat* 467 *Śrāvaṇa vadi* 4 *Śrī-Jayarājadevasya rāja krtya Sarva-sammatena saṃvat* 467 *Vaiśākha sudi* 7 (folio 28). (With the consent of both the royal houses, Jayarājadeva was made king on the 4th day of Śrāvaṇa, dark fortnight, in the year 467 N. E., and on the 7th day of Vaiśākha, right fortnight, 467 N. E., with the consent of all) –The Sanskrit portion of the Bendall Vaṁśāvalī, (folio 28).

was nominated and thus the first of a new line, is described as *Puṣyābhiṣeka,* and this used to take place in *Gwāla,* the modern Deo Pāṭan, which was then the capital city.

Also, the Bendall Vaṁśāvalī gives evidence to the effect that Pāṭan was not the then capital, as believed by Prof. Petech and D. R. Regmi. During the days of the Licchavis and the Thakuris, Hāḍigāon,[13] the modern Viśālnagar, was the capital and the modern Māligāon and the adjoining area called Taṅgāl were the sites, where the palaces of historic Mānagṛha and Kailāśakūṭa stood. When the capital was moved to Deo Pāṭan, we do not know, yet a guess may here be hazarded that it was done about the time when the Paśupati bhaṭṭāraka Saṃvatsara was started, which is none other than the Nepal Era corresponding to 880 A. D., after Viśālnagar was consumed by a big fire as legend would have it.

At a particular site in Taṅgāl, while digging recently for a septic tank to be made, many large earthen bricks have been unearthed bearing in Licchavi script the name of Aṁśuvarman saying *"Śrī mahāsāmantāṁśuvarmaṇaḥ".* The wall, which was discovered at a level which is more than 10 feet underground, probably belonged to a building raised by Aṁśuvarman. One out of every ten or twelve bricks, measuring $14 \times 9 \times 2^1/_2$ inches, bear the inscription embossed on one side of it. The site is located at a close distance from the Māneśvarī shrine, to the north-east. The pond where the annual festival of Viśālnagar takes place lies at close distance to the north of the site.

It is a pity that interest in archaelogy is still lacking in this country, since a Rāṇa, who owns this site and who had discovered those bricks while digging for a septic tank to be made for this new building, wants to keep it private, and like him many others who had built their dwellings around the site before, too, have kept quiet. It is a known fact that even while digging for the building of the Taṅgāl Durbar, a Rāṇa palace, early in this century, many such materials of archaelogical interest were discovered, but none took interest in them.

This locality is called *Māgaa* (*Māgala*) in Newari, and *Māligāon,* a corrupt form of *Mānigāon* or *Mānagāon,* in Nepali, and the adjoining area to the north is called Taṅgāl. It did not occur, it seems, to Prof. Petech that this *Māgaa* or *Māgala* in Newari and *Māligāon* in Nepali also can be corrupt forms of *Mānagṛha,* when he says:—

"The mediaeval centre of Patan was *Māṇigal,* the modern *Maṅgal* Bazār. It seems to me that there is a strong likelihood that the name *Māṇigal* goes back to *Mānagṛha* and that the two sites are identical. Newari *gal* is the equivalent of Sanskrit *Gṛha:* and *Māni* or *Māṇi* cannot be a corruption of *Mani,* jewel,

13. Spelt as Harigaon by Prof. Sylvain Lévi in his work 'Le Népal'

Bricks discovered at Taṅgal/Māneśvarī, Kāṭhmaṇḍu
Map of the Taṅgal-Haḍigāon-Māligāon area, East of Kāṭhmaṇḍu

because the first vowel is always, without exception, written as long. *Māni* and *Māna* have the same root as and are presumably connected with the goddess *Māneśvarī,* who from the beginning to the end was placed in a special relationship with the royal houses of Nepal. It must not be concealed that a local tradition seems to place *Mānagṛha* in the neighbourhood of Deo Patan, but it is difficult to assess its value. Until positive evidence to the contrary is forth coming, I still incline to identify old Mānagṛha with the emplacement of the modern royal palace of Patan".

Māgaa, Māgala can be a corrupt form of *Mānagṛha* and likewise *Māṇigal,* the modern *Maṅgal* Bazār in Pāṭan. But since the *Mānagṛha* at Pāṭan seems to have been built much later, when Pāṭan as Lalitapuri became the capital a few centuries after, of an *ardha rājya* or half kingdom[14], as evidenced by the Bendall *Vaṁśāvalī,* we can safely assume that this was named simply after the older *Mānagṛha* palace at *Māgaa* or *Māligāon* near Taṅgāl. The close vicinity of *Māgaa* or *Māligāon* and *Taṅgāl* in this area, and the closeness likewise of *Maṅgal* and *Taṅgāl* in Pāṭan suggests that Pāṭan or Lalitapuri, as it is called in the *Vaṁśāvalī,* and which was a later kingdom partitioned from the bigger and older kingdom of Nepal, named its palaces after the older ones. Obviously, a new *Mānagṛha* and a new Kailāśakūṭa had then come into being in the half kingdom of Lalitapuri; the former, being the palace of nominal kings and the latter, the palace of de-facto rulers. The sites of these came to be known as *Manigla* and *Tanigla* respectively in the later Malla times and now as *Mangaa* and *Tangaa* corresponding to *Māgaa* and *Taṅgāl* in Viśālnagar area.

14. *rāja Srī-Vijayadeva varṣa* 31 *tena lalitāpurī ardha-rājyaṃ karoti*
(King Vijayadeva ruled the half kingdom of Lalitapuri for 31 years C. 1000 A.D.)
–The Skt. portion of the Bendall *Vaṁśāvalī,* (folio 23).

Notes on the Topography of Present Day Haḍigāon

Niels Gutschow

The discovery of a brick, bearing the name of Aṁśuvarman, certainly throws a new light on the history of Hāḍigāon. Since the reading of the inscription on the Garuḍa stele of Satya Nārāyaṇa close to the former bank of the Rudramatī by Lévi[1] the village had closely been connected with the time of the early Ṭhākurīs.

Naraḥ and Magaḥ form two distinctly separated Newar settlements on a ridge 10–12m. above the Rudramatī (Newari- Hijā khusī) which in former times ran very close to Satya Nārāyaṇa and Maiti Dyaḥ. The India-Tibet route probably did cross the river at the site of Satya Nārāyaṇa, transgressing the ridge through Naraḥ and passing by Nyalma pūkhū just west of Hāḍigāon. From there, traces of the former road have disappeared due to the construction of the Taṅgāl Darbar by the end of the 19th century. From Nāg Pokharī in Naksāl again down to the Toraṇ Bhavan (at present the Chinese Embassy) we are able to trace the ancient road which would lead straight to Asan ṭol of Kāṭhmāṇḍu, were it not blocked again by a Rāṇa Darbar (Lāl Darbar, built 1890–1892 by Bir Shumsher).

Both the settlements have the typical infrastructure of a Newar town: a *pīṭh* as the 'seat' of a mother gooddess in the open country and a *dyocheṁ* inside the settlement. A *dyocheṁ* serves as a sort of community house which provides space for people to held a feast, and which houses the icon of that god or goddess to which the aniconic *pīṭh* is related. The icon in the *dyocheṁ* is solely worshipped by a *pūjārī,* whereas the *pīṭh* is the place of daily worship by the people. The icon will be carried to the *pīṭh* in a *khaṭ* during the yearly festival (*yātra*) and will visit all the lanes of the settlement in a chariot (*rath*). In Naraḥ, the chariot is not disassembled but kept as a whole in a garage-like building.

These notes were discussed with Ṭhākurlāl Mānandhar on the spot in August 1976. Repeated field surveys in 1974–1976 were made possible by the generous grants of the 'Deutsche Forschungsgemeinschaft'. Moreover, I owe thanks to the Nepal Research Centre for manifold assistence.

1. Sylvain Lévi, Le Népal, Vol. II, Paris 1905
   see also : HMG, Kathmandu Valley, Vol. II, Wien 1975, p. 103

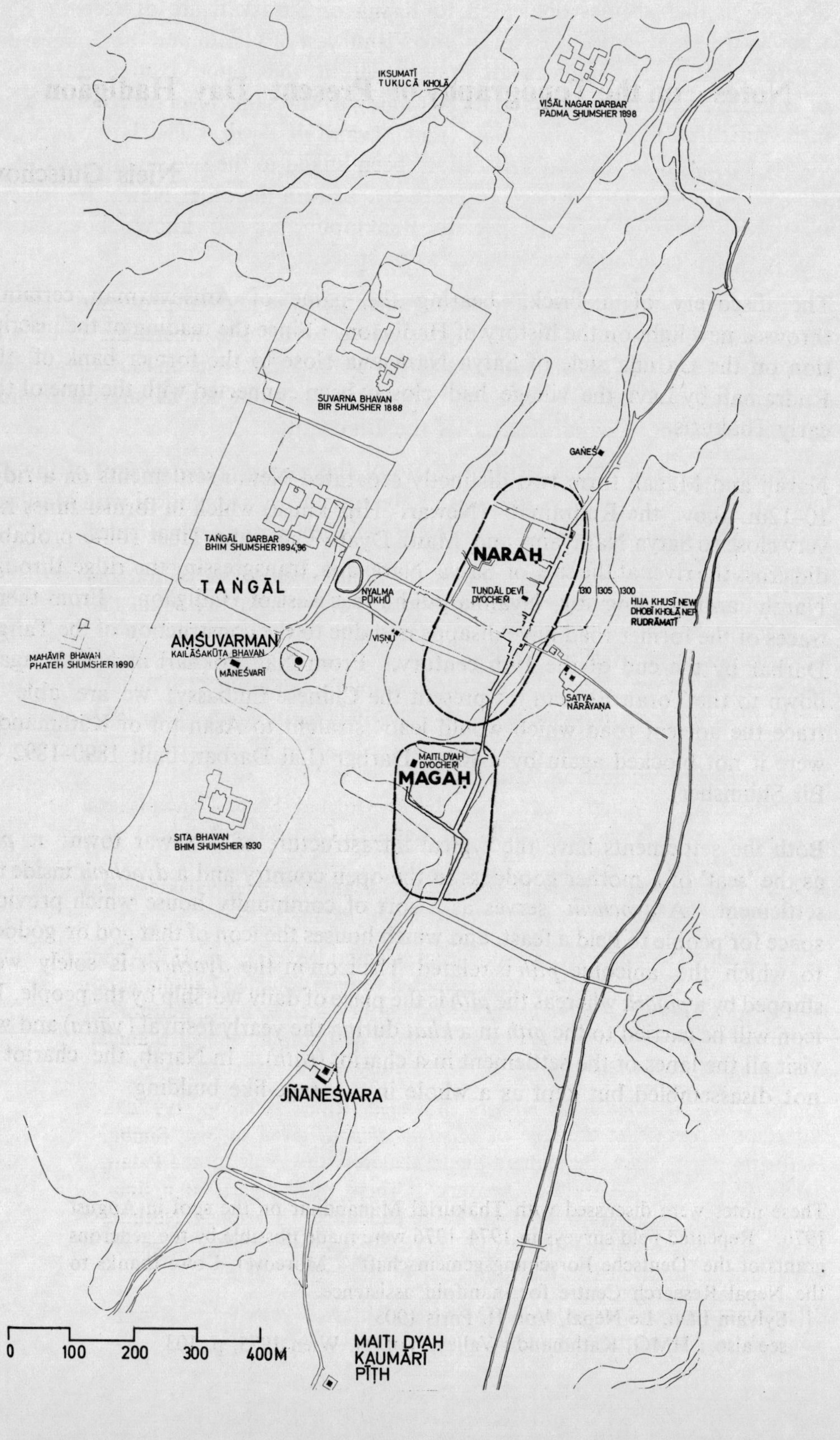
IKSUMATĪ
TUKUCĀ KHOLĀ
VIŚĀL NAGAR DARBAR
PADMA SHUMSHER 1898
SUVARNA BHAVAN
BIR SHUMSHER 1888
GAṆEŚ
TAṄGĀL DARBAR
BHIM SHUMSHER 1894,96
NARAḤ
TAṄGĀL
NYALMA
PUKHŪ
TUNDĀL DEVĪ
DYOCHEṀ
1310 1305 1300
HIJA KHUSĪ NEW
DHOBĪ KHOLĀ NEP
RUDRĀMATĪ
AṀŚUVARMAN
KAILĀŚAKŪṬA BHAVAN
MĀNEŚVARĪ
VIṢṆU
MAHĀVIR BHAVAN
PHATEH SHUMSHER 1890
SATYA
NĀRĀYAṆA
MAITI DYAḤ
DYOCHEṀ
MAGAḤ
SITA BHAVAN
BHIM SHUMSHER 1930
JÑĀNEŚVARA
0 100 200 300 400M
MAITI DYAḤ
KAUMĀRĪ
PĪṬH

Several smaller shrines dedicated to Kṛṣṇa or Sarasvatī are of recent origin, whereas the Gaṇeś north of Naraḥ, the Viṣṇu west of Naraḥ and the Jñāneśvara[2] together with his Unmatta Bhairava (within the same compound) south of Magaḥ, are to be considered as belonging to the same level of original ritual infrastructure like Maiti Dyaḥ and Tvaṃraḥ Dyaḥ. The latter two goddesses have by way of 'sanskritization' been linked to the two manifestations of Durgā, Kaumārī and Vaiṣṇavī respectively. From the other Newar settlements of the Kāṭhmāṇḍu Valley, especially Bhaktapur[3], we do know about the importance of the Mātṛkās as guardians of space.

Another site is likely to provide an argument for the ancient provenance of the area under discussion. The Māneśvarī close to the site where the brick was found was the *Digudyo* (lineage god) of the Malla kings. It is an esoteric goddess about which not much is known. The location alone let us suggest to link it with the ancient Ṭhākurī capital of the 7th century.

Were the site of the brick really the site of the palace (*Kailāśakūṭa*) of the defacto ruler Aṁśuvarman, Naraḥ were to be considered as identical with Madhyalakhu,[4] the capital with the palace (*Mānagṛha*) of the formal ruler.

2. Jñāneśvara is one of the 64 *Mahādevas,* which encircle the central and most important holy place (*tīrtha*) of Nepal, Paśupatināth, in a spiral-like form.
   see : Bhāṣā Vaṁśāvalī, 1 (2020), pp. 6–8
   or : T. W. CLARK, "The Rāṇī Pokharī Inscription, Kathmandu" in Bulletin of the School of Oriental and African Studies, Vol. XX, London 1957, pp. 167–187

3. For preliminary information see :
   Niels GUTSCHOW and Bernhard KÖLVER, Ordered Space Concepts and Functions in a Town in Nepal, Nepal Research Centre Publications Vol. I, Wiesbaden, 1975
4. According to the Vaṁśāvalī edited by WRIGHT, Madhyalakhu was founded by Aṁśuvarman, who left Deva Pāṭan.

   see : Daniel WRIGHT, History of Nepal, Cambridge 1877, p. 133. About half a century later Bīradeva was supposed to have founded Lalitpur south of Madhyalakhu. Although legends cannot be taken to prove a historical process, it seems not likely that the palace of Lalitpur, named Mānigal, is identical with Mānagṛha of the 7th century as PETECH suggests.

Luciano PETECH, Mediaeval History of Nepal, Rome 1958, pp. 199–200. BURLEIGH proves that the title of *Manigaladhipati,* given to Siva Simha, Harihara Simha and Siddhinara Simha denotes their rule in the Patan, palace (end of 16th/early 17th century). These titles appear at a time, when the basic pattern of present day Patan had already developed. Nothing can be said therefore about the location of the Thakuri or early Malla palace nor can it be connected to the Managrha of the early Thakuris.

Peter BURLEIGH, "A Chronology of the Later Kings of Patan" in Kailash Vol. IV, No. 1, Kathmandu 1976, p. 30.

In fact, topography makes the site, which is 200m. beyond the settlement, and divided from it by a 5 m. deep ditch, an ideal site for the palace of the de-facto ruler Aṁśuvarman. Madhyalakhu – high above the watered plains of the Rudramatī, and Kailāśakūṭa in a respectable distance – a hypothesis which to prove we need more evidence. Evidence which only archaeology will provide.

Puṣyābhiṣeka

Mahes Raj Pant

It is known from the *Gopālarājavaṁśāvalī* and other historical documents of Nepal that some of the Nepalese kings who reigned in the period between 1167–1381, underwent a consecration known as *puṣyābhiṣeka.* But the term *puṣyābhiṣeka* does not seem to have yet been defined authentically by anyone in the context of Nepalese history. For this reason, this paper is prepared to define the term *puṣyābhiṣeka* on the basis of the *śāstra*-s.

There is a separate *Pariśiṣṭa* captioned *Puṣyābhiṣeka* in the *Ātharvaṇapariśiṣṭa* which gives details of the rite of *puṣyābhiṣeka.* This helps us to know the meaning of *puṣyābhiṣeka.* It is written in the *Pariśiṣṭa* that the king should receive *puṣyābhiṣeka* while the moon is in conjunction with the asterism *Puṣya,* and that the king who has undergone the rite on the asterism *Puṣya* will enjoy pleasure in both worlds :

अथ पुष्याभिषेकस्य विधिं वक्ष्यामि साम्प्रतम् ... ॥५.१.१॥
पुण्याहं वाचयित्वास्य आरम्भं कारयेद् बुधः ।
तिष्यनक्षत्रसंयुक्ते मुहूर्ते करणे शुभे ॥५.४.२॥
अथर्वविहितो ह्येष विधिः पुष्याभिषेचने ।
राजा स्नातो महीं भुङ्क्ते शक्रलोकं स गच्छति ॥५.५.७॥[1]

"Now I describe the rite of *puṣyābhiṣeka.* Having solemnized *puṇyāhavacana,* the learned man shall get it begun when the moon is in conjunction with the *Pusya* astereism and there are auspicious *karaṇa* and *muhūrta.* The rite of *puṣyābhiṣeka* is prescribed in the *Atharvaveda.* The king, who has taken bath [in this way] enjoys the earth and goes to Indra's world[2]."

Bhaṭṭotpala, the celebrated commentator of Varāhamihira, quotes copiously from both Vṛddhagarga and Garga in his commentary on the *Bṛhatsaṁhitā.*

* This paper, originally written in Nepali, was published in *Pūrṇimā,* IX (V. S. 2032 [1975]), pp. 13–27. Subsequently it was translated into English with slight additions and modifications by the author himself.

1. *Ātharvaṇapariśiṣṭa* V. [*The Pariśiṣṭas of the Atharvaveda,* edited by George Melville Bolling and Julius von Negelein (Leipzig : Otto Harrassowitz, 1909), pp. 66–68.]

2. The translations are my own.

According to Vṛddhagarga, the Devas were defeated by the Daityas in war, and an *abhiṣeka* for Indra, the king of the Devas, was performed by Bṛhaspati, the preceptor of the Devas, on his own asterism *Puṣya*. Indra, having become powerful by virtue of the *abhiṣeka*, triumphed over the Daityas. Since then *puṣyasnāna* is being observed:

तथा च वृद्धगर्गः ।

देवाश्च दितिजैः[3] सार्धं स्पर्धमाना हि मानिनः ।
परस्परं महद् युद्धं चक्रुः सर्वे सुरासुराः ॥
ततो दैत्यगणैः क्रुद्धैर्देवाः सर्वे विनिर्जिताः ।
ततोऽङ्गिराः सुरगुरुर्ध्यानसक्तोऽभवत् पुरा ॥
पुरन्दराभिषेकार्थं बृहस्पतिरकल्पयत् ।
तिष्यमात्मीयनक्षत्रं यस्य देवो बृहस्पतिः ॥
तेन चैवाभिषिक्तश्च देवराजः पुरन्दरः ।
ततो बलसमारूढो नाशयामास दानवान् ॥
देवाश्च हृष्टमनसः पुरीं प्राप्यामरावतीम् ।
पुष्यस्नानं बलतरं तदारभ्य प्रवर्तितम् ॥[4]

"In like manner Vṛddhagarga says :
The haughty Devas vied with the Daityas. All the Devas and Daityas fought each other fiercely. All the Devas were defeated by the angry Daityas. Then Bṛhaspati, the preceptor of the Devas, engaged himself in meditation. Bṛhaspati resolved to perform an *abhiṣeka* on his own asterism *Puṣya* of which the presiding deity is Bṛhaspati himself. Then Indra, the king of the Devas, being anointed on that asterism became endowed with strength and destroyed the Daityas. The Devas, glad at heart reached the city of Amarāvatī (abode of the Devas). Since then *puṣyasnāna* is being observed."

According to Garga, human beings and animals residing in the kingdom of the one who is anointed on every *Puṣya* will not undergo any suffering :

तथा च गर्गः । प्रतिपुष्येण यो राजा स्नायीत विधिपूर्वकम् ।
तस्य राष्ट्रे न सीदन्ति मर्त्या ये जन्तवो भुवि ॥[5]

"In like manner Garga says:
Human beings and animals do not perish in the kingdom of the one who shall duly take bath on every *Puṣya*."[6]

3. Erroneously देवाश्चावितिजैः is printed in the Dvivedī edition.
4. Vṛddhagarga quoted in the commentary of Bhaṭṭotpala on the *Bṛhatsaṁhitā* 47.2. [*The Bṛihat Saṁhitā by Varāhamihira with the Commentary of Bhaṭṭotpala,* edited by Sudhákara Dvivedí (Benares: E. J. Lazarus and Co. 1895, 1897), p. 581.]
5. Garga quoted in the commentary of Bhaṭṭopala on the *Bṛhatsaṁhitā* 47.84. [Sudhákara Dvivedí, *op. cit.* p. 603.]

There is a separate *adhyāya* entitled *Puṣyasnānādhyāya* in the *Bṛhatsaṁhitā* by Varāhamihira, in which the rite of *puṣyasnāna* is explained in detail. It greatly helps us to understand the meaning of the term *puṣyābhiṣeka*. It states that *puṣyasnāna* received by the king on every *Puṣya* will increase his pleasure, fame and wealth. Varāhamihira permits its observance on asterisms other than *Puṣya* itself, but he says that the *puṣyasnāna* held on other asterisms can yield only half the result of that which is performed on the *Puṣya* asterism. It is written in the *Bṛhatsaṁhitā* that the *puṣyasnāna* performed on the full moon day of the month of Pauṣa yields greater result. According to Varāhamihira, the king should receive *puṣyasnāna* at times of public calamity, eclipses, on seeing comets and at times of planetary conflicts. Varāhamihira also writes that the king who wishes for overlordship and for the birth of a son should undergo the rite of *puṣyasnāna* on the occasion of his coronation. He also states that the *puṣyasnāna* performed for the elephants and horses will make them immune from diseases. He has also written something about the antiquity of the *puṣyasnāna* tradition. He tells us that the rite of *puṣyasnāna* was taught by Brahma to Bṛhaspati for the sake of Indra and later, the rite was known to Vṛddhagarga who imparted it to Bhāguri. According to Varāhamihira he put down in the *Bṛhatsaṁhitā* the rite of *puṣyasnāna*, following **Vṛddhagarga's** instruction to Bhāguri :

या व्याख्याता शान्तिः स्वयम्भुवा सुरगुरोर्महेन्द्रार्थे ।
तां प्राप्य वृद्धगर्गः प्राह यथा भागुरेः शृणुत ।।२।।
पुष्यस्नानं नृपतेः कर्तव्यं दैववित्पुरोधोभ्याम् [7] ... ।।३।।
आदावनडुहश्चर्म जरया संहृतायुषः ।
प्रशस्तलक्षणभृतः प्राचीनग्रीवमास्तरेत् ।।४३।।
ततो वृषस्य योधस्य चर्म रोहितमक्षतम् ।
सिंहस्याथ तृतीयं स्याद् व्याघ्रस्य च ततः परम् ।।४४।।
चत्वार्येतानि चर्माणि तस्यां वेद्यामुपास्तरेत् ।
शुभे मुहूर्ते सम्प्राप्ते पुष्ययुक्ते निशाकरे ।।४५।।
एतत् प्रयुज्यमानं प्रतिपुष्यं सुखयशोऽर्थवृद्धिकरम्
पुष्याद् विनार्धफलदा पौषी शान्तिः परा प्रोक्ता ।।८२।।
राष्ट्रोत्पातोपसर्गेषु राहोः केतोश्च दर्शने ।
ग्रहावमर्दने चैव पुष्यस्नानं समाचरेत् ।।८३।।
अधिराज्यार्थिनो राज्ञः पुत्रजन्म च काङ्क्षतः ।
तत्पूर्वमभिषेके च विधिरेषः प्रशस्यते ।।८५।।
अनेनैव विधानेन हस्त्यश्वं स्नापयेत् ततः ।
तस्यामयविनिर्मुक्तं परां सिद्धिमवाप्नुयात् ।।८७।।[8]

विष्णुधर्मोत्तरे,

पुष्यस्नानं तथा कुर्यात् प्रतिमासं नराधिपः ।

"It is written in the *Visnudharmottara* :
The king shall have *pusyasnana* every month."

6. The *Viramitrodaya* quotes the *Visnudharmottara* which states that the king should receive *pusyasnana* every month :

   Viramitrodaya Rajanitiprakasa [*Viramitrodaya, Rajniti Prakasa, by Mahamahopadhyaya Pandita Mitra Misra,* edited by Bishnu Prasad (Benares: Chowkhamba Sanskrit Series Office, 1916), p. 115.]

7. Erroneously दैववितुपरोधाभ्याम् is printed in the Dvivedí edition.
8. *Bṛhat-saṁhitā* 47. [Sudhákara Dvivedí, *op. cit.* pp. 581, 594, 603,604.]

"Listen to the propitiatory rite which was explained by Brahma to Bṛhaspati for the sake of Indra and getting which, Vṛddhagarga told the same to Bhāguri. *Puṣyasnāna* of a king must be performed by the astrologer and the priest. The priest shall first spread the hide of a bull which had in its body auspicious signs and had died ageing, with the neck part turned towards the east. Then he shall spread also the unimpaired red hide of a bull trained for fighting. Then the third hide must be that of a lion. Then the hide must be that of a tiger. The priest shall spread these four hides on the altar when the moon is in conjunction with *Puṣya* and there is an auspicious *muhūrta*. This bath performed on every *Puṣya* increases happiness, fame and wealth. This bath performed without the presence of *Puṣya* gives only half the result. This rite performed on the day when the full moon is on *Puṣya* is said to be superior. The king shall have *puṣyasnāna* on occurrences of *utpāta*[9] and *upasarga* in the country, eclipses, comets and planetary conflicts. This rite is commendable at the time of *prathamābhiṣeka* (coronation)[10] of the king wishing for overlordship and for the birth of a son. Then the king shall cause the elephants and horses to be bathed according to this rite. They, being immune from diseases, will attain the highest perfection."

9. For *utpāta* see *adhyāya* 45 (*utpatādhyāya*) of the *Bṛhatsaṁhitā* [Sudhákara Dvivedí, *op. cit.* pp. 539-570.]
10. *Rājābhiṣeka* (coronation) was known as *pūrvābhiṣeka* or *prathamābhiṣeka* and, the *abhiṣeka* performed annually when the moon is on the same asterism as that on which *rājābhiṣeka* was performed is known as *saṃvatsarābhiṣeka*

Vīramitrodaya, Rājanītiprakāśa [Vishnu Prasâd, *op. cit.* p. 115] :

विष्णुधर्मोत्तरे,

संवत्सराभिषेकं च कथयस्द महीक्षितः । ...
राजाभिषेकनक्षत्रे प्रतिसंवत्सरं द्विजः ।
पूर्वाभिषेकविधिना कर्त्तव्यमभिषेचनम् ॥

"It is witten in the *Viṣṇudharmottara :*
Tell me the *saṃvatsarābhiṣeka* of the king.
Following the rite of *pūrvābhiṣeka, abhiṣeka* must be performed each year by the Brahmin on the same asterism as that on which *rājābhiṣeka* was performed."

The same passage is quoted in the *Rājadharmakaustubha* 53.
[See *Rājadharmakaustubha of Anantadeva,* edited by Kamala Kṛṣṇa Smṛti-tīrtha (Baroda : Oriental Institute, 1935), p. 379.]

Śrī 5 *Mahārājādhirāja-Gīrvāṇayuddhavīravikrama-Śāhadevaviracitā Sat-karmaratnāvalī*, [The Satkarmaratnāvalī by His Majesty King Gīrvāṇayuddhavīravikrama Śāhadeva], edited and published by Rāmanātha Ācārya and Damodara Koiralā, vol. II (Kathmandu, V. S. 2029 [1972]), pp. 494, 516.

अथ राज्याभिषेकः ॥
स द्विधा प्रथमाभिषेकः सांवत्सरिकश्चेति ।
इति प्रथमराज्याभिषेकः ।

"Here is the description of *rājyābhiṣeka.*
There are two kinds of *rājyābhiṣeka* viz. *prathamābhiṣeka* and *saṃvatsar-ābhiṣeka.* Here ends the description of *prathamarājyābhiṣeka.*"

The rite of *pusyasnana* is elaborately described in the *Kalikapurana* in a whole *adhyaya*. Also this *adhyaya* makes explicit the meaning of the term *pusyabhiseka*. It is stated that the king should receive *pusyasnana* in the month of Pausa when the moon is in conjunction with the asterism *Pusya,* and that it brings benefit and wards off the dangers of famine and death. The *Kalikapurana* gives alternative times for *pusyasnana*. It permits the performance of *pusyasnana* on the asterism *Pusya* when the *tithi* is *tritiya* and when day is either Sunday, Tuesday or Saturday, irrespective of whether it happens on unauspicious *Karana*-s like *Bhadra* and *yoga*-s like *Vyaghata, Vaidhrti, Vajra, Sula* or *Harsana* and tells us that *pusyasnana* held at such a time removes all the defects. It is also stated in the *Kalikapurana* that *pusyasnana* is permissible even under the harmful influence of the planets and the occurrences of *iti* (which means excessive rains, drought, attack by locusts, rats, parrots and foreign invasions) in months other than Pausa if the moon is in conjunction with *Pusya*. It tries to establish the antiquity of the tradition of *pusyasnana,* stating that Brahma explained the *pusyasnana* rite to Brhaspati for the felicity of all the Devas, including Indra. The *Kalikapurana* mentions that the coronation and also the investiture of the office of an heir-apparent should be performed according to the rite of *pusyasnana* :

श्रृणु राजन् प्रवक्ष्यामि पुष्यस्नानविधिक्रमम् ... ॥१॥
पौषे पुष्यर्क्षगे चन्द्रे पुष्यस्नानं नृपश्चरेत् ।
सौभाग्यकल्याणकरं दुर्भिक्षमरणापहम् ॥२॥
विष्ट्यादिदुष्टकरणे व्यतीपाते च वैधृतौ ।
वज्रे शूले हर्षणादौ योगे तु यदि लभ्यते ॥३॥
तृतीयायुक्तपुष्यर्क्षं रविसौरिकुजेऽहनि ।
तदा समस्तदोषाणां तत् स्नानं हानिकारकम् ॥४॥
ग्रहदोषाश्च जायन्ते यदि राज्येषु चेतयः ।
तदा पुष्ये तु नक्षत्रे कुर्यान्मासान्तरेऽपि च ॥५॥
इयं तु ब्रह्मणा शान्तिरुद्दिष्टा गुरवे पुरा ।
शक्रादिसर्वदेवानां शान्त्यर्थम् ... ॥६॥
अनेनैव विधानेन नृपतेभिषेचनम् ॥१४२॥
युवराज्याभिषेकश्च कुर्याद् राजपुरोहितः ॥१४३॥[11]

"O King, listen to the the rite of *puṣyasnāna* which I tell you.

The king shall have *puṣyasnāna* which brings good fortune and well-being and wards off famine and death, when the moon is in conjunction with the *Puṣya* asterism. If taken, in *Pauṣa* on the third lunar day and on Sunday, Tuesday or Saturday when the moon is in conjunction with the *Puṣya* asterism inspite of the unauspicious *Karaṇa*-s like *Bhadrā* and *yoga*-s like *Vyatīpāta, Vaidhṛti, Vajra, Śūla* or *Harṣana*, the bath removes all blemishes. The king shall have *puṣyasnāna* in other months too, when the moon is in conjunction with the *Puṣya* in case there are evil omens due to planetary positions and there is *iti* (which means excessive rains, drought, attack by locusts, rats, parrots and foreign invasions). In olden times this propitiatory rite was told by Brahma to Bṛhaspati for the felicity of all the Devas, including Indra. The royal priest shall perform the coronation and the investiture of the office of an heir-apparent according to this rite."

11. *Kālikāpurāṇa* 86. [*Kālikāpurāṇam*, edited by Biśwanārāyaṇ Śāstrī (Varanasi: Chowkhamba Sanskrit Series Office, 1972) pp. 635, 644.]

It is known from the *Gopālarājavaṁśāvalī*, the *Kaiser Fragment of Vaṁśāvalī* and a copper-plate inscription from the Indreśvara Temple, Panauti that *puṣyābhiṣeka* was performed for eight Nepalese kings, viz. Rudradeva, Someśvaradeva, Guṇakāmadeva, Jayabhīmadeva, Jayaśīhamalla, Anantamalla, Jayārimalla and Jayārjunadeva.

सम्वत् २६७ पौषकृष्णत्रयोदश्यां, शुक्लदिने, श्रीरुद्रदेव, पुष्याभिषेक कृतवान् राज्ये ॥
पुष्याभिषेकात तुषारवृष्टि च भवति ॥[12]

"On Friday, the 13th day of the dark half of Pauṣa, in the year 267[13] Śrī-Rudradeva had *puṣyābhiṣeka* in the kingdom. By reason of *puṣyābhiṣeka* there was also snow-fall.

12. *The Kaisher Fragment of Vaṁśāvalī*, Kaiser Library MS. No. 171 (hereafter VK) p. 7. The whole text of VK is published by Luciano Petech, *Mediaeval History of Nepal* (C. 750–1480) (Rome : Istituto Italiano per il Medio ed Estremo Oriente, 1958) pp. 213–217 and by D. R. Regmi, *Medieval Nepal,* pt. III (Calcutta : Firma K. L. Mukhopadhyay, 1966) pt. II, pp. 158–163. We have an unpublished reading of VK established by Ramaji Tevari, *et al.* of Saṁśodhana-maṇḍala in 1959. Verifying the original MS. I have improved the reading and I like to give the correct reading of the relevant passages of VK throughout this paper.]

13. According to VK *puṣyābhiṣeka* of Rudradeva took place on Friday, the 13th day of the dark half of Pauṣa, in N. S. 267. But the date verified does not correspond to calculation, since the 13th day of the dark half of Pauṣa was a Wednesday, not a Friday. We therefore have to deal with this problem in some detail.

We know that in N. S. 265 Narendradeva was reigning in Nepal :

श्रीमत् राजाधिराज परमेश्वरः परमभट्टारकः श्री नरेन्द्रदेव विजयराज्ये । सम्वत् भानु ५[२६५]

Palm–leaf MS. *Pañcarakṣā,* in the personal collection of Dharma Bahadur Maharjan, Dupata Tole, Patan. [Hemaraj Sakya and T. R. Vaidya, *Medieval Nepal* (*Colophons and Inscriptions*) (Kathmandu : T. R. Vaidya, 1970) Colophon No. 6, p. 12]:

"In the year 265, during the victorious reign of Śrīmān Rājādhirāja Parameśvara Paramabhaṭṭāraka ŚrīNarendradeva."

Ānandadeva ascended the throne on the 1st day of the dark half of Māgha, in N. S. 267 :

माघकृष्णसुचन्द्रमाप्रतिपदे सप्ताधिके षष्टिके,
काले वर्षशतद्वये शुभदिने, राज्यं वरप्रापितो ।
श्रीनेपालाः समस्तमण्डलमहीत्राता प्रजानासम्यक्
पीड्यं शास्त्रं तदा सुनिर्मितगुणे श्रीनंददेवप्रभुः ॥

राजा श्रीआनन्ददेव ...

Gopālarājavaṁśāvalī (hereafter GRV) National Archives, Kathmandu I. 1583, fol 24 b, lines 4–5, fol, 25 a, [The Sanskrit portion of GRV from folio 22b, line 5 to folio 29a, line 5 is published by Petech, *op. cit.* pp. 219–224. The whole text of GRV is published by Yogī Naraharinātha, "Gopāla-vaṁśāvalī (571 Varṣa aghi Lekhiyeko Itihāsa)" [Gopāla-vaṁśāvalī– A Chronicle Written 571

Years Ago], *Himavat-saṁskṛti* I, no. 1 (V. S. 2016 [1959], pp. 9–25 and by Regmi, *op. cit.* pp. 112–157. We have an unpublished reading of GRV deciphered by Ramaji Tevari, *et al.* of Saṁśodhana-maṇḍala in 1959 from the photo (Kaiser Library MS. No. 730) of the original MS. The passage quoted above is published by Bhola Nath Paudel, "Ānandadeva, Rudradeva ra Amṛtadevako Samayamā Eutā Vicāra" [An Investigation into the Time of Ānandadeva, Rudradeva and Amṛtadeva]", *Pūrṇimā*, I, no. 3, (V. S. 2021 [1964]), p.19. Verifying the original MS. I have improved the reading and I like to give the correct reading of the relevant passages of GRV throughout this paper.]

"On Monday, the 1st day of the dark half Māgha in the year 267, on an auspicious day, the lord Śrī[Ā]nandadeva obtained the kingship. He was virtuous, the guardian of the whole Nepālamaṇḍala and remover of the miseries of the subjects. He ruled according to the *śāstra*s-.

King ŚrīĀnandadeva..."

The date is accurate. On that Monday *Pratipad* lasted for 60 *ghaṭī*-s and 56 *pala*-s.

We find Ānandadeva mentioned as reigning king up to the 2nd day of the bright half of Kārtika, N. S. 287:

श्रीमदानन्ददेवस्य विजयराज्ये सम्वत् २८७ कार्तिक सुदि २ ...

MS. *Aṣṭasāhasrikā Prajñāpāramitā* belonging to a vihāra, by name, Ombahal in Patan. [D. R. Regmi, *Medieval Nepal,* pt. 1 (Calcutta : Firma K. L. Mukhopadhyay, 1965) p. 178]

"In the victorious reign of ŚrīĀnandadeva, on the 2nd day of the bright half of Kārtika in the year 287''

We find Rudradeva mentioned as reigning king from the 8th day of the dark half of Phālguna, N. S. 288 :

सम्वत् २८८ फाल्गुनकृष्णाष्टम्याम् ... रुद्रदेवस्य विजयराज्ये

An inscription engraved on one of the fountains of Vajrayoginī, Sankhu [Paudel, *op. cit.* p. 25.]

"On the 8th day of the dark half of Phālguna, in the year 288, in the victorious reign of Rudradeva."

We find Rudradeva mentioned as reigning king up to the 15th day of the bright half of Mārga, N. S. 295 :

महाराजाधिराजश्रीरुद्रदेवस्य राज्ये । सम्वत् २९५ आग्रहणपूर्ण्णमास्यां आदित्यदिने

MS. *Bhagavatyāḥ Prajñāpāramitāyāḥ Ratnaguṇasañcayagāthā*, Asiatic Society of Bengal, n. 10736. [Paudel, *op. cit.* p. 26.]

"In the reign of Mahārājadhirāja ŚrīRudradeva. On Sunday, on the 15th day of the bright half Mārga, in the year 295."

The date is accurate. On that Sunday *Pūrṇimā* lasted for 40 *ghaṭī*-s and 40 *pala*-s.

VK's statement that the *puṣyābhiṣeka* of Rudradeva took place on the 13th day of the dark half of Pauṣa, in N. S. 267 cannot be regarded as authentic, since in N. S. 265 Narendradeva was reigning, and we have the proof that Ānandadeva who ascended the throne on the 1st day of the dark half of Māgha, in N. S. 267, was reigning up to the 2nd day of the bright half of Kārtika, N. S. 287 and

सम्वत् २९९ कार्त्तिके कृष्णषष्ठि शुक्लवार । रा [ज्जा श्री]सोमेश्वरदेव, पुष्याभिषेक कृतवान् ॥[14]

"On Friday, the 6th day of the dark half of Kārtika, in the year 299[15] King ŚrīSomeśvaradeva had *puṣyābhiṣeka*."

राजा श्रीगुणकामदेव पुष्याभिसेष[16] कृत्य[17]

"King ŚrīGuṇakāmadeva having *puṣyābhiṣeka*"...

only after that comes the mention of Rudradeva as the king from the 8th day of the dark half of Phālguna, N. S. 288 through the 15th day of the bright half of Mārga, N. S. 295. So it appears that 267 was inadvertently written for 287 in VK. This conjecture is proved by calculation, since the 13th day of the dark half of Pauṣa in N. S. 287 was a Friday and the day for the *puṣyābhiṣeka* of Rudradeva is given as Friday in VK. As is now confirmed, *puṣyābhiṣeka* of Rudradeva took place on the 13th day of the dark half of Pauṣa, in N. S. 287.

Luciano Petech (Petech, *op. cit.* p. 68) writes about the date of Rudradeva's *puṣyābhiṣeka* as follows :

According to VK the coronation (*puṣyābhiṣeka*) of Rudradeva took place in 267 *Pauṣa kṛṣṇa* 13. The date is impossible, as it is too early. So 267 must be mistake for 287 and the date corresponds to January 5th, 1167. ...

D. R. Regmi (Regmi, *op. cit.* pp. 182-183) writes about the date of Rudradeva's *puṣyābhiṣeka* as follows :

The authority of VK puts the initial year of his reign in *Pauṣa* 267 (*Kṛṣna* 13). But this date is at least twenty years earlier as the colophon dates of the last reign prove. If it is a mistake for 287 Pauṣa Kṛṣṇa 13 corresponding to January 5th 1167, then this would give correct date for his accession because we know that about this time Ānandadeva had died.

Both Petech and Regmi are right in stating that the date of *puṣyābhiṣeka* of Rudradeva given in VK as N. S. 267 does not seem correct for it is impossible for Rudradeva to be reigning in N. S. 267, hence the date 267 of VK is wrongly written for N. S. 267. But both Petech and Regmi are wrong in asserting that the 13th day of the dark half of Pauṣa, N. S. 287, corresponds to January 5th, 1167. The date actually corresponds to January 20, 1167.

14. VK p. 8.
15. The date given in VK is accurate and on that Friday *Ṣaṣṭhī* lasted for 6 *ghaṭī*-s and 28 *pala*-s.
16. The reading of the term *puṣyābhiṣeka* which is found in GRV is spelt in two ways. Some have spelt the word as *puṣyābhiṣeka* (Cecil Bendall, "Historical introduction", p. 8 in Hara Prasād Śāstrī, *A Catalogue of Palm-leaf and Selected Paper Manuscripts belonging to the Durbar Library, Nepal,* vol. I (Calcutta, 1905), Petech, *op. cit.* pp. 221–223); and some others as *puṣpābhiṣeka* (Dhanabajra Bajracharya, "Nepālakhaldomā Tehraute [Harasiṁhadevako] Ākramaṇa Viṣayako Vicāra [Investigation into the Tirhutia (of Harasiṁhadeva) Invasion of Kathmandu Valley]", *Itihāsa–saṁśodhana,* no. 7 (V. S. 2013[1957]), p. 7, Yogī Naraharinātha, *op. cit.* p. 12, Gautamvajra Vajracharya, "Prādhyāpaka ŚrīTotrarāja Pāde tathā ŚrīGuru Paṃ. Nayarāja

राजा श्रीगुनकामदेव, पुष्याभिख[क] कृतवान् ॥ सम्वत् ३०५ पौषशुदि ७ अंगवासरे ॥[18]

"King ŚrīGuṇakāmadeva had *puṣyābhiṣeka* on Tuesday, the 7th day of the bright half of Pauṣa, in the year 305."

पुष्याभिषेक राजा श्रीजयभीमदेव[19]

"King ŚrīJayaBhīmadeva, for whom *puṣyābhiṣeka* was performed."

पुष्याभिषेक राजा श्रीजयशीह्मलदेव[20]

"King ŚrīJayaŚīhamalladeva, for whom *puṣyābhiṣeka* was performed."

पुष्याभिषेक राजा श्रीअनन्तमलदेव[21]

"King ŚrīAnantamalladeva, for whom *puṣyābhiṣeka* was performed."

Panta Viracita "Nepālako Saṃkṣipta Itihāsa" mā tathā Aru Itihāsakaraharūka Granthamā Rahekā Aśuddhiko Saṁśodhana [The Correction of Errors Contained in *Nepālako Saṁkṣipta Itihāsa* (Short History of Nepal) by Prof. Totra Raj Pandey and Revered Guru Pt. Naya Raj Pant and in the works of other Historians]", *Itihāsa-saṁśodhana*, no. 54 (V. S. 2019 [1963]), Dhanabajra Bajracharya *et al.*, *Itihāsa-saṁśodhanako Pramāna-prameya* [*The Gist of Itihāsa-saṁśodhana*] (Patan: Jagadamba-prakasana, V. S. 2019 [1962]), main pt. p. 334, Dhanabajra Bajracharya, "Ḍoyaharu Ko Hun ?" [Who are the Ḍoya ?]", *Pūrṇimā*, I, no. 4 (V. S. 2021) [1965], p. 23, D. R. Regmi, Medieval Nepal pt. III, pt. i, pp. 121-122, Dhanabajra Bajracharya, "*Rājyābhiṣekako Aitihāsika Mahatva* [Historical Importance of Coronation]", *Contribution to Nepalese Studies,* II, no. 1, (1975) p. 5). It therefore was necessary to me to decide the correct reading of the term after the consultation of the manuscript of GRV. Though the word on the original manuscript looks to be *puṣyābhiṣeka*, the conjunct ष्य as contained therein looks like ष्प at some places. Therefore it is difficult to say for certain that GRV actually has the form *puṣyābhiṣeka,* and not *puṣpābhiṣeka*. Notwithstanding this I prefer the form *puṣyābhiṣeka* to *puṣpābhiṣeka*, as it is in conformity with the *śāstra*-s].

17) GRV fol. 25b, line 2

18. VK p. 8.

19. GRV fol. 26a, line 1.
20. GRV fol. 26a line 3.
21. GRV fol. 26a, line 5.

तदनन्तरे श्रीजयतुङ्गमलदेवस्य आत्मजः श्रीजयरुद्रमलदेवस्य प्रभुतेन स्वकुटुम्बश्रीजयारिमलदेवस्य पुष्याभिषेकं कृत्यः राजा भक्तिमात्रन्ददौ,[22]

"Hence ŚrīJayaRudramalladeva, son of ŚrīJayaTuṅgamalladeva performed *puṣyābhiṣeka* for his own kinsman ŚrīJayārimalladeva by dint of his influence and gave him only his loyalty."

अनन्तरे जयतुङ्गमल्लस्य, आत्मजः श्रीजयरुद्रमल्लदेवस्य प्रभूतेन, स्वकुटुंब, श्रीजयारिमल्लदेव, पुष्याभिषेकं कृत्य, रा[ज]भुक्तिमात्रं ददौ ॥[23]

"Afterwards, ŚrīJayaRudramalladeva performed *puṣyābhiṣeka* for his own kinsman ŚrīJayārimalladeva and allowed him only to enjoy the kingdom."

अत्रासीज्जयसिंहरामनृपतिः प्रख्यात भूमण्डले
श्रीमान् श्रीभगवान् शिवः पशुपतिर्येन प्रतिष्ठापितः ।
येनैवापि जयार्ज्जुनो नरपतिः पुष्याभिषेकः कृतो
येनासौ स्थितिराजमल्लनृपतिः पट्टाभिषेकीकृतः॥[24]

"Here was king JayaSiṁharāma who was well-known in the world. By him the [image of] lord Paśupati was consecrated. By him *puṣyābhiṣeka* for King Jayārjuna was performed. By him *paṭṭābhiṣeka* for King Sthitirājamalla was performed."

In as much as the availability of the dates of the *puṣyābhiṣeka* held for three Kings viz. Rudradeva, Someśvaradeva and Guṇakāmadeva, amongst the eight kings for whom *puṣyābhiṣeka* was held, helps us to have an idea about the nature of *puṣyābhiṣeka*, which was then in vogue in Nepal.

It is already stated that the first available material on the reign of Rudradeva is dated the 8th day of the dark half of Phālguna, N. S. 288 and his *puṣyābhiṣeka* was performed on the 13th day of the dark half of Pauṣa, in N. S. 287. The first available material on the reign of Someśvaradeva is dated the 6th day of the bright half of Mārga N. S. 299 [25]. As already mentioned, his *puṣyābhiṣeka*

22. GRV fol. 27a line 5, fol. 27b, line 1.
23. VK p. 11.
24. A copper-plate inscription at Indreśvara temple, Panauti consecrated in the memory of JayaSiṁharāma. [Ramaji Tevari *et al.* "JayaSiṁharāmako Saṃjhanāmā Rākhieko Panautī Indreśvara-mandirako Tāmrapatra [A Copper-plate Inscription at Indreśvara Temple Panauti Consecrated in the Memory of JayaSiṁharāma]", *Pūrṇimā* IV, V. S. 2024 [1967], pp. 130–133. Yogī Naraharinātha, "Jayasiṁha Rāmako Kanakapatra [The Copper-plate Inscriptition of Jayasiṁha Rāma]", *The Gorkhapatra,* August 9, 1969. The term is spelt as *puṣpabhiṣeka* both in *Pūrṇimā* and *The Gorkhapatra.* However, in the rubbing of this inscription deposited in Saṁśodhana-maṇḍala, I am not able to distinguish a difference between प and य. Notwithstanding this, I prefer the form '*puṣyābhiṣeka*' to '*puṣpābhiṣeka*', as it is in confirmity with the *śāstra*-s].
25. MS. *Prāyaścittopadeśa*, Kaiser Libray MS. No. 522. [Petech, *op. cit.* p. 70, Regmi, *op. cit.* pt. I, p. 187. The colophon quoted below is verified against the original] :

सम्वत्सरे नवाधिका, नवति, शतद्वये, मासे मार्ग्गशिरशुक्लषष्ठमे । राजाधिराजपरमेश्वरः रघुकुलतिलक-श्रीसोमेश्वरदेवस्य विजयराजे...

was performed on the 6th day of the dark half of Kārtika in N. S. 299. The first available material on the reign of Guṇakāmadeva is dated N. S. 306.[26]

"On the 6th day of the bright half of Mārga, in the year 299. In the victorious reign of Rajādhirāja Parameśvara ŚrīSomeśvaradeva, the best of the family of Raghu."

26. MS. *Manthānabhairavatantra*, National Archives, II 218 :

श्रीमद् गुणकामदेव संपूज्य नेपालदेशराज्ये। स्वस्तिसंवत् ३०६

"In the kingdom of Nepāl which is being enjoyed by ŚrīGunakāmadeva. The year 316".

Petech (*op. cit.* p. 73) reads the colophon quoted above as follows: *Śrīmad-Guṇakāmadeva-sambhujya Nepāladeśa rakṣva svasti saṃvat* 316.

Petech (*op. cit.* p. 73) writes about the colophon as follows:
The last digit could also be read 4, but certainly not 9, as in the handwritten catalogue of the Darbar Library.

Regmi (Medieval Nepal, pt. 1, pp. 193–194) reads the colophon as follows: *Śrīmad-Guṇakāmadeva sambhujya Nepāladeśe rājye svasti saṃvat* 306.
Regmi (*op. cit.* p. 194) writes about the colophon as follows. : Petech (doc. 3) says that the last digit could be read as 4 but he read the middle figure as 1 so that the date was rendered 316; the middle digit, however, looks definitely to be 0 and the last must be 6.

In the printed catalogue of the National Archives the colophon is given as follows:

श्रीमद्गुणकामदेव संभुज्य नेपालदेश राज्य ॥ स्वस्ति संवत ३०६ ॥

ŚrīNepālaRāṣṭrīyābhilekhālayastha Hastalikhitapustakānāṃ Bṛhatsūcīpatram [The Master Catalogue of the Manuscripts Deposited in the National Archives], vol. IV, pt. II (Kathmandu : Rāṣṭrīya Abhilekhālaya, V. S. 2025 [1969]), p. 56.

The year is deciphered as 316 by Petech and as 306 by Regmi and the Pandits of the National Archives. When I verifed it against the original I found that the year read by Regmi and the Pandits was correct. So I have published the year as 306. The correct text of the colophon, as verified against the original, as has already been given.

On the regnal year of Guṇakāmadeva,T.R. Vaidya writes as follows :
Colophon No. 9 pushes back the regnal year of Guṇakāmadeva by one year from N. S. 306 to 305. The present manuscript confirms the evidence of the *Kaisar Vaṁśāvalī* (f. 18) which gives N. S. 305 *Pauṣa Sudi* 7 *Angaravara*... as the date of his coronation.

Hemaraj Sakya and T. R. Vaidya, *Medieval Nepal* (*Colophons and Inscriptions*) (Kathmandu : T. R. Vaidya, 1970),introduction p. XII.

On the date of Colophon No. 9 Sakya and Vaidya (*op. cit.* p. 17) write as follows :

We have already mentioned that *puṣyābhiṣeka* for him was performed on the 7th day of the bright half of Pauṣa, in N. S. 305. Therefore it appears that the *puṣyābhiṣeka* mentioned in the Nepalese documents is a kind of coronation, because the dates of the *puṣyābhiseka* ceremony of all the kings are earlier than the first available materials on those kings. In the light of the *Bṛhat-saṁhitā,* which states that it is advisable to perfom the rite of *pusyasnāna* during coronation, and in that of the *Kālikāpurāṇa*, which states that the coronation is to be observed, according to the *puṣyasnāna* rite and as well as of popularity of those texts in Nepal in the Malla period[27], it seems to us that the *puṣyābhiṣeka* for those kings was performed as the ritual of the coronation.

Date: Saṃvat 305, in the reign of Raja Gunakamadeva.
The colophon No. 9 is read by Sakya and Vaidya as follows :
Sakya and Vaidya, *op. cit.* p. 18. MS. *Aṣṭasāhasrikā Prajñāpāramitā,* deposited in Oku Bahal, Patan.

ये धमहितु प्रभवा हेतुत्तेषान्तथागतो ह्यवदत् ।
तेषाञ्चयो निरोध एवं वादीमहाश्रमणः ।। ।।

शरर्दित्रिशते ... ... धिगते दशमी गुरूवासर योगवरे पृथु पुण्ययो धृत्वतिवामकरे ।। राज्य श्रीगुणकामदेव जयिनो राजेर्केऽर्क सद्धर्म जीक्ष प्रन्तत्रलि ... ... प्रज्ञापारमितेयमग्र जननी साद्धवरूग्मैवरैः शाक्यः शासन सः ... ...

How Sakya and Vaidya arrived at a conclusion from this passage that Guṇa-kāmadeva was the king in N. S. 305 is not clear to me. The numerals of the year in this colophon were written out in words. But some letters have disappeared after the phrase शरदि त्रिशते which means in the year three hundred. Thus it is clear that in the colophon only the words denoting the numeral in the hundredth place are clear and the words denoting the numerals in the tenth and unit places have disappeared.
Regmi (Regmi, *op. cit.* p. 193) has published the colophon before Sakya and Vaidya did. Although Regmi somewhat differs from Sakya and Vaidya in the reading, he also has given only the words denoting the numeral in the hundredth place. He has not commented on the year of the colophon. His reading is as follows:
Śaraditriśati... dhiravi gate daśamī guruvāsare Yogavāre prīthupuṇyapāyoh... vāmakare– rājye Guṇakāmadeva jayino rājye etc. etc.
Since the colophon does not prove that Guṇakāmadeva was reigning in N. S. 305, we have to recognize the above colophon, dated N. S. 306, as the first available material on the reign of Gunakāmadeva for the time being.

(All the dates quoted here are worked out by Dinesh Raj Pant.)

27. In the printed catalogue of the National Archives three palm-leaf manuscripts of the *Bṛhatsaṁhitā* in Newari script are described (*Nepāla-RājakīyaVīrapustakālayathahastalikhitapustakānāṃ Bṛhatsūcīpatram* [The Master Catalogue of Manuscripts Deposited in Durbar Library], vol. I (Kathmandu: Vīrapustakālaya, V. S. 2017 [1960] pp. 132b-138). In the same catalogue (pp. 137–138) four paper manuscripts of the *Bṛhat-saṁhitā* in Newari script are described. Besides these the three paper manuscripts of the *Bṛhatsaṁhitā* in Newari script are deposited there (IV. 1683, V. 3510 and 7719). In the Kaiser Library a paper manuscipt of the *Bṛhat-saṁhitā* written in Newari script is deposited (No. 401) .

It is clearly known from the quotations from the *śāstra*-s, which have been referred to above, that this *abhiṣeka* was designated as *puṣyābhiṣeka* because it was performed particularly when the moon was in conjunction with the asterism *Puṣya*. In spite of this, the variant of the term *puṣyābhiṣeka* which is *puṣpābhiṣeka* was also in use.[28]

Owing to the importance given to the asterism *Puṣya* as an auspicious time for the coronation, the royal chariot meant for the coronation was called as *puṣyaratha*.[29] Later, people forgot the real meaning of *puṣyaratha* and started accepting the *puṣparatha* as the variant of *puṣyaratha* and distorted its meaning as a chariot as tender as flower[30]. Similiarly the variant of the phrase

In the printed catalogue of the National Archives 12 paper manuscripts of the *Kālikāpurāṇa* in Newari script are described (Bābukṛṣṇa Sharmā, *Rāṣṭrīyābhilekhālayasthahastalikhitapracīnapustakānāṃ Bṛhatsūcīpatram* (The Master Catalogue of the old Manuscripts Deposited in the National Archives), vol. VIII (Kathmandu : Rāṣṭrīya Abhilekhālaya, V. S. 2025 [1965]), pp. 34–39, 339.) Besides these three paper manuscripts of the *Kālikāpurāṇa* are deposited in the National Archives (I. 958 and 1017, IV. 2675). In the Kaiser Library a paper manuscript of the *Kālikāpurāṇa* written in Newari script is deposited (No. 371). It is worth mentioning here that the oldest extant manuscript of the *Kālikāpurāṇa* is in Newari script written in N. S. 202 (See Karel Rijk van Kooij, *Worship of the Goddess according to the Kālikāpurāṇa* (Leiden : E. J. Brill, 1972), p. 3, n. 4) which is 85 years earlier than the first reference to *puṣyābhiṣeka* in Nepalese history.

28. In *The Pariśiṣṭas of Atharvaveda* p. 69 *puṣpābhiṣeka* is, in a footnote, given as the variant of *puṣyābhiṣeka*. *Chaturvarga Cintâmaṇi by Hemādri*, vol. II, edited by Bharatachandra Śiromaṇi *at al.* (Calcutta : The Asiatic Society of Bengal, 1879) deals with *puṣyasnāna* on pp. 600–628 wherein at only one place (p. 600) the form *puṣpābhiṣecanam* is printed. In *Vīramitrodaya Rājnītiprakāśa*, pp. 112–114 the passage relating to *puṣyābhiṣeka* is quoted from the *Ātharvaṇapariśiṣṭa*, wherein at two places *puṣpābhiṣeka* and in at three places *puṣyābhiṣeka* is printed. In *Rājadharmakaustubha of Anantadeva* pp. 375–377 the passage relating to *puṣyabhiṣeka* is quoted from the *Ātharvaṇapariśiṣṭa* wherein at one place (p. 375) the variant of *puṣyābhiṣeka* is given as *puṣpābhiṣeka* in a footnote. The same passage from the *Ātharvaṇapariśiṣṭa* is quoted in *Satkarmaratnāvalī* vol. II, pp. 516–518 where *puṣpabhiṣeka* is printed throughout the chapter.

29. See my "Puṣyaratha" in *Journal of Nepal Research Centre* vol. 1
30. Bhānujī Dīkṣita on *Amarakośa* 2.8.51. [The *Nâmaliṅgaanuśâsana* (*Amarakosha.*) *of Amarasiṃha* (*with the Commentary*) *Vyâkhyâsudhâ or Râmâśramî. of Bhânujî Dîkṣit*, 5th edition, edited by Śivadatta, revised by Wasudev Laxman Śâstrî Paṇśîkar) Bombay : Nirṇaya-sâgar Press, 1929) p. 283

तिष्यनक्षत्रसंयुक्ते मुहूर्ते करणे शुभे (when the moon is in conjunction with the *Puṣya* asterism and there are auspicious karaṇa and muhūrta) employed in the *Ātharvaṇa-pariśiṣṭa*[31] was also in use as तिथिनक्षत्रसंयुक्ते मुहूर्ते करणे शुभे (in an auspicious *tithi, karaṇa* and *muhūrta*). It seems to us that the permission given in the *Bṛhat-saṁhitā* and in the *Kālikāpurāṇa* to perform *puṣyasnāna* on other asterisms than the *Puṣya* also helped to forget the correct reading of *pusyābhiṣeka*. In the *Satkarmaratnāvalī*: अयं चाभिषेकः प्रतिवर्षं महानवम्यां कर्तव्यः । पुष्पाभिषेको महानवम्याम् । इत्याथर्वणसूत्रात्[32] (Annually this *abhiṣeka* ought to be performed on the *Mahānavamī* day. It is said in the *Atharvanasūtra* that *puṣpābhiṣeka* must be performed on *Mahānavamī*) and the precept regarding *puṣyābhiṣeka* is entitled there as अथ प्रतिवर्षाभिषेकः[33] (Here is the description of the annual *abhiṣeka*); it can be conjectured that the rite of *puṣyābhiṣeka* was used in other purposes, too.

Nevertheless the compilers of the enormous Sanskrit-German dictionary, generally known as St. Petersburg Lexicon, were not able to decide the *puṣpasnāna* as the variant of *puṣyasnāna* and were confused with the meaning of *puṣpasnāna*[34]. It was Monier Monier-Williams who decided that the *puspa-*

भसाविति । पुष्य इव रथः । पुष्ये यात्रोत्सवादौ रथो वा । अन्तस्थमध्यः । पकारमध्यपाठे तु पुष्पमिव रथः इति विग्रहः । एकं युद्ध बिना यात्रोत्सवादौ सुखभ्रमणार्थस्य रथस्य ।

"पुष्य इव रथः, that means the chariot as the asterism *puṣya* or पुष्ये यात्रोत्सवादौ रथो वा, that means the chariot meant for procession and festival, etc. The semi-vowel य is in the middle of the word *pusyaratha*. In the form *puṣparatha* accepting प् in the middle of the word *puṣparatha* the separation of the compound word *puṣparatha* is पुष्पमिव रथः that means the chariot which is as tender as flower. This single word is for the chariot used for processions, festivals and pleasure trips at times of peace."

31. In *The Pariśiṣṭas of the Atharvaveda* p. 69 *Tithinakṣatra-saṃyukte* is a variant of *Tiṣyanakṣatrasaṃyukte*. In *Chaturvarga Chintāmaṇi by Hemadri* vol. II p. 618 तिथिनक्षत्रसंयुक्तमुहूर्तंकरणे शुले is printed for तिष्यनक्षत्रसंयुक्ते मुहूर्ते करणे शुभे. In *Vīramitrodaya Rājanītiprakāśa* p. 114, *Rājadharma–Kaustubha* p. 366 and *Satkarmaratnāvalī* vol. II p. 517 तिथिनक्षत्रसंयुक्ते मुहूर्ते करणे शुभे is printed for तिष्य नक्षत्रसंयुक्ते मुहूर्ते करणे शुभे.

32. Satkarmaratnāvalī, vol. II, p. 518

33. *op. cit.* p. 516

34. Otto Böhthlingk and Rudolph Roth, *Sanskrit– Wörterbuch* [Sanskrit Dictionary] vol. IV (St. Petersburg : Buchdruckerei der Kaiserlichen Academie der Wissenschaften, 1865) Column 822 :
पुष्पस्नान (पु°+स्नान) n. Blumenbad, eine Art Weihe (अभिषेक): पुष्पस्नानं नृपतेः कर्तव्यं दैववित्पुरोधोभ्याम् । नातः परं पवित्रं सर्वोत्पातान्तकरमस्ति VARÂH. BṚH. S. 47,3.38. पुष्पस्नानाम्बुभिः सपुष्पैः ॥ अभिषिञ्चेन्मनुजेन्द्रं पुरोहितोऽनेन मन्त्रेण ॥ 54. 83.77,23. Der Schol. hat पुष्यस्नान vor sich gehabt, da er das Wort durch पुष्यनक्षत्रेण स्नपनम् erklärt; पुष्यस्नान hat auch KÂLIKÂ–P. nach dem ÇKDR.

"पुष्पस्नान (पु°+स्नान) n. flowerbath, a kind of consecration (अभिषेक). पुष्पस्नानं नृपतेः कर्तव्यं दैववित्पुरोधोभ्याम् । नातः परं पवित्रं सर्वोत्पातान्तकरमस्ति ॥ Varāhamihira's *Bṛhatsaṁhitā* 47.3.38.

snāna as the variant of *puṣyasnāna,* and *puṣpābhiṣeka* as the variant of *puṣyābhiṣeka.* He was aware of the real meaning of the four variants as *puṣpasnāna, puṣyasnāna*, the *puṣpābhiṣeka* and *puṣyabhiṣeka* which he stated as "a particular ceremony of purification performed while the moon is passing through the asterism *pusya*"[35]. Inspite of this, some Nepalese historians, not knowing the real

पुष्यस्नानाम्बुभिः सपुष्पैः ॥ अभिषिञ्चेत्मनुजेन्द्रं पुरोहितोऽनेन मन्त्रेण ॥ 54.8.3.77,23 . Explaining the word through पुष्यनक्षत्रेण स्नपनम्, the scholiast had before him पुष्यस्नान. पुष्यस्नान also occurs in the *Kālikā-Purāṇa* which is referred to in *Śabdakalpadruma.*"

op. cit. column 824:

पुष्यस्नान (पु° + स्नान) n. eine best. zur Zeit, da der Mond in Sternbilde Pushja steht, stattfindende Reinigungscerimonie : पौषे पुष्यर्क्षगे चन्द्रे पुष्यस्नानं नृपश्चरेत् । सौभाग्यकल्याणकरं दुर्भिक्षमरकापहम् ॥ KÂLIKÂ-P. 89 in ÇKDR.–Vgl. पुष्पस्नान.

पुष्याभिषेक (पुष्य + अभि°) m. dass. ebend. und PARIÇ. in Verz. d. B. H. 90, 4.–vgl. पुष्पाभिषेक.

पुष्यस्नान पुष्पस्नान (पु° + स्नान) n. "An auspicious purification ceremony which takes place when the moon stands on puṣya asterism : पौषे पुष्यर्क्षगे चन्द्रे पुष्यस्नानं नृपश्चरेत् । सौभाग्यकल्याणकरं दुर्भिक्षमरकापहम् *Kālikā-purāṇa* 89 which is refered to in शब्दकल्पद्रुम. cf. पुष्यस्नान. पुष्याभिषेक (पुष्य + अभिषेक) m. same meaning ibid. and in *Pariśiṣṭa* which is referred to in Albrecht Weber, *Die Handschriften–Verzeichnisse der Königlichen Bibliothek* [The Catalogue of the Manuscripts Deposited in the Royal Library] (Berlin: 1853) 90,4."

35. Monier Monier-Williams, *A Sanskrit–English Dictionary* (Delhi: Motilal Banarsidass, 1963 [Photo reprint of 1899 edition], pp. 639–640:
pushpa–snāna, n., v. l. for *Pushya-sn°* …
Pushya–snāna, n. a partic. ceremony of purification preformed while the moon is passing through the asterism P°, Var. (v. l. *pushpa-s°*)
Pushyābhiṣeka, m. id., ib. (v. l. pushpabh°). —
Since the compilers of the St. Petersburg Lexicon write that Varāhamihira gives the form *puṣpasnāna* in his *Bṛhat-saṁhitā* and Monier–Williams writes that Varāhamihira has given the variant *puṣpasnāna* in his *Bṛhatsaṁhitā*, we have to deal with this question in some detail.

We have already mentioned that there are three palm–leaf manuscripts of the *Bṛhat-saṁhitā* in Newari script in the National Archives, Kathmandu. But I could not find in the Archives all the manuscripts except IV. 162 wherein we can see the form *puṣyasnāna* clearly. As already stated, there are seven paper manuscripts of the *Bṛhat-saṁhitā* in Newari script in the Archives. I was fortunate enough to find all the manuscripts except one (I. 1195). In two of the six manuscripts I did not find (I.281 and V. 7719) the *Puṣyasnānādhyāya*. In the remaining four manuscripts (I.15 and 217, IV. 1683 and V. 3510) the form *puṣyasnāna* is clearly visible. In the first volume of the catalogue of the National Archives (p. 38) it is mentioned that there is a paper manuscript of Bhaṭṭotpala's commentary upon the *Bṛhatsaṁhitā* in Devanāgarī script (I. 293) in the Archives, but it could not be found there. But I found there four paper manuscripts of the *Bṛhatsaṁhitā* in Devanāgarī script (1.238, V. 571,575 and 6154). In one of these manuscripts (V. 575) I could not find *puṣyasnānādhyāya.* On the basis of the orthography of other three manuscripts it is impossible to distinguish between the conjuct ष्प and ष्य. So I am unable to say definitely whether it is written as *puṣpasnāna* or *puṣyasnāna.* We have already mentioned the existence of a paper manuscript of the *Bṛhatsaṁhitā* in Kaiser

meaning of the term *puṣyābhiṣeka,* have interpreted it as "anointment flowers"[36], which is totally wrong.

Library wherein I could not distinugish between conjuct प and य. I found a paper manuscript of the *Bṛhatsaṁhitā* in Devanāgarī script, (no. 274), in the Kaiser Library where in *puṣyasnāna* is clearly visible. In a paper manuscript of the *Bṛhat-saṁhitā* copied in Gorkha in Devanāgarī script in Shaka 1599 during the reign of Pṛthvipati Śāha (Dinesh Raj Pant, "Gorakhali Rājāharūkā Rājyakāla [The Regnal Years of the Kings of Gorkha]", *Pūrṇimā*, IX, (V. S. 2031 [1974])), wherein I could not distinguish between conjunct प 'pa' and य 'ya'.

Of the printed editions of the *Bṛhat-saṁhitā* I have cousulted five editions viz. *Bṛhat-saṁhitā,* edited by H. Kern (Calcutta : The Asiatic Society of Bengal, 1865), *Bṛhat-saṁhitā,* edited by Jibananda Vidyasagar, (Calcutta, 1880), Sudhākara Dvivedī, *op. cit.*, *ŚrīmadVarāhamihirācāryapraṇīta Bṛhatsaṁhitā*,, edited and translated into Hindī by Baladevaprasāda Miśra (Bombay: Lakṣmī Veṅkaṭeśvara Press, 1897), *VarāhamihiraviracitāBṛhatsaṁhitā*, edited with Hindī commentary by Acyutānanda Jhā, (Benaras: The Chowbhamba Vidya Bhawan, 1959). The form *puṣyasnāna* is printed in the editions of Kern, Dvivedī, Miśra and Jhā. In the edition of Vidyāsāgara, however, the form *puṣpasnāna* is printed only at one place while the form *pusyasnāna* is printed throughout the book. Vaman Pandurang Kane, *History of Dharmaśāstra* vols. I– V (Poona: Bhandarkar Oriental Research Institute, 1930–1962) and Ajaya Mitra Shastri, *India as seen in the Bṛhatsaṁhitā of Varāhmihira* (Delhi, Patna, Varanasi: Motilal Banarsidass, 1969) also spell *puṣyasnāna*.
Following Monier-Williams, the compilers of the Greatest Hindi Lexicon write as follows:
Śyāmasundaradāsa *et. al.*, *Hindī Śabda–Sāgara* [The Ocean of the Hindī Words] (Banares: Kāśī-Nāgarī-Pracariṇī Sabhā, 1914–1922) pp. 2166–2167 :

पुष्पस्नान ... "देखो पुष्यस्नान" ।

पुष्यस्नान ... विघ्न शांति के लिये एक स्नान जो पूस के महीने में चंद्रमा के पुष्य नक्षत्र में होने पर होता है। यह स्नान राजाओं के लिये है। कालिकापुराण और बृहत्संहिता में इस स्नान का पूरा विधान मिलता है।

Puṣpasnāna n. m. (sanskrit) see Puṣyasnāna.
Puṣyasnāna n. m. (sanskrit)

A bath for the removal of obstacles which is performed in the month of Pauṣa when the moon is in conjunction with the *Puṣya* asterism. This bath is for kings. In the *Kālikāpurāṇa* and the *Bṛhat-saṁhitā* the whole precept of this bath is available.

36. Dhanabajra Bajracharya "Rājyābhiṣekako Aitihāsika Mahatva [Historical Importance of Coronation]", *Contributions to Nepalese Studies*, vol. II, no. 1 (1975), pp. 4, 5] :

गोपालवंशावलीमा पुष्पाभिषेक गरिएका राजाहरूको लामो सूची परेको छ। ... आथर्वणपरिशिष्टमा "पुष्पाभिषेक" गर्ने विधान दिइएको छ। यस विधानको अन्त्यमा पुरोहितद्वारा मन्त्रिएको पुष्प आदि माङ्गलिक वस्तु राजाको शिरमा राखिने हुनाले यो अभिषेक "पुष्पाभिषेक" कहलिएको हो।

"In the *Gopālavaṁśāvalī,* there is a long list of kings for whom *puṣpābhiṣeka* was performed. In the *Āthavarṇa-pariśiṣṭa* the rite of *puṣpābhiṣeka* is given. Since, at the end of this rite, flowers and other auspicious objects consecrated with the *mantras* are placed on the head of the king by the *priest*, it is called "*puṣpabhiṣeka*"."

Gautamvajra Vajracharya, "The Coronation of the Kings Nepal", *The Rising Nepal,* Feburary 20, 1975 :
"There were two kinds of royal consecration, the one known as pushpa– or pushya-abhiseka (purification ceremony literally "anointment with flowers"), the other pattabhiseka or pattabandha (coronation ceremony) . . . Unfortunately, no contemporary descriptions of it are preserved although the popularity in Nepal of such texts as the Kalika-purana and Varamihira's Vrihat-samhita wherein the pushpabhisheka is described suggests that this was also the method followed in Nepal.

Puṣyaratha*
The Royal Chariot for Coronation

Mahes Raj Pant

Six kinds of chariots, including *pusyaratha,* are mentioned in the *Rathadhyaksa-prakarana* of the *Kautaliya Arthasastra:*

देवरथपुष्यरथसांग्रामिकपारियाणिकपरपुराभियानिकवैनयिकांश्च रथान् कारयेत् ॥[1]

"The superintendent of chariots shall cause to be made *devaratha*, *puṣyaratha, saṅgrāmikaratha, pāriyāṇikaratha, parapurābhiyānikaratha* and *vainayikaratha."*[2]

Since this passage is not explicit enough to give us a clear idea of the kind of chariot known as *puṣyaratha,* we have to ascertain the meaning of *puṣyaratha* from other texts. At first, let us try to find out the meaning of *puṣyaratha* on the basis of the well-known sanskrit lexicon Amarakośa:

याने चक्रिणि युद्धार्थे शताङ्गः स्यन्दनो रथः ।
असौ पुष्यरथश्चक्रयानं न समराय तत् ॥[3]

"The wheel-carriage for war is known as *śatāṅga, syandana* or *ratha*. The wheel-carriage, which is not meant for war, is known as *puṣyaratha."*

* This paper, originally written in Nepali, was published in *Pūrṇimā,* Saṁśodhana-maṇḍala, Kathmandu's journal of Nepalese history and Sanskritic studies, IX, (V. S. 2032) [1975], pp. 8–12. Subsequently, it was translated into English with slight modifications by the author himself.

1. *Kauṭalīya Arthaśāstra* II. 33.5. [*Arthaśāstra of Kauṭilya. A New Edition*, by J. Jolly and R. Schmidt, vol. 1 (Lahore: Moti Lal Banarsi Dass, 1923), p. 82.]

2. The translations, except where specified, are my own.

3. *Amarakośa* II. 8. 51. [*The Nāmaliṅgānuśāsana* (*Amarakosha*) *of Amarasiṁha with the Commentary* (*Vyākhyāsudhā or Rāmāśramī*) *of Bhanuji Dikshit,* 5th edition, edited with notes by Śivadatta, revised by Wāsudev Laxmaṇ Śāstrī Paṇśīkar (Bombay: Nirnaya - sagar Press, 1929), pp. 282–283.]

It appears from this passage that the wheel-carriage used for other purposes than war is known as *puṣyaratha.*

Saṅgrāmikaratha is one of the six kinds of chariots which are mentioned by Kauṭalya. The word *saṅgrāmika,* i.e. capable of being used in war, is formed by affixing *ṭhañ* after *saṅgrāma* meaning "war"[4]. So it seems that Kauṭalya used the word *saṅgrāmikaratha* for the war – chariot.

Daśaratha thought of handing over the state powers to Rāma after the performance of Rāma's *yauvarājyābhiṣeka* (investiture of the office of heir-apparent) and accordingly preparations were made for the ceremony. Owing to the manipulation of his step-mother, on the very day which was fixed for his *abhiṣeka* ceremony, Rāma was commanded for exile to the forest instead of receiving the *abhiṣeka.* Then he went back home saying good-bye to all. The distraught appearance of Rāma and absense of any regal insignia on him made Sītā suspicious and her making inquiries are mentioned in the *Valmīkīya Rāmāyaṇa.* In those sentences uttered by Sītā as described by Vālmiki, *puṣyaratha* also is mentioned along with other royal insignia. The passage reads as follows:

> अद्य बार्हस्पत : श्रीमान् युक्तः पुष्यो नु राघव ।
> प्रोच्यते ब्राह्मणैः प्राज्ञैः केन त्वमसि दुर्मनाः ॥
> न ते शतशलाकेन जलफेननिभेन च ।
> आवृतं वदनं वल्गु छत्रेणाभिविराजते ॥
> व्यजनाभ्यां च मुख्याभ्यां शतपत्रनिभेक्षणम् ।
> चन्द्रहंसप्रकाशाभ्यां वीज्यते न तवाननम् ॥
> वाग्मिनो[5] बन्दिनश्चापि प्रहृष्टास्त्वां नरर्षभ ।
> स्तुवन्तो नाद्य दृश्यन्ते मङ्गलैः सूतमागधाः ॥
> न ते क्षौद्रं च दधि च ब्राह्मणा वेदपारगाः ।

4. *Kāśikā* V. 1. 101. [*Kāśikā. A Commentary on Pāṇini's Grammar,* edited by Aryendra Sharma, *et al.* (Hyderabad: Sanskrit Academy, Osmania University, 1969–1970) p. 490]:

तस्मै प्रभवति सन्तापादिभ्य :

तस्मै इति चतुर्थीसमर्थेभ्यः सन्तापादिभ्य : प्रभवति इत्यस्मिन् विषये ठञ् प्रत्ययो भवति । समर्थः, शक्त : प्रभवति इत्युच्यते । अलमर्थे चतुर्थी । सन्तापाय प्रभवति, सान्तापिकः । सान्नाहिकः ।

सन्ताप । सन्नाह । सङ्ग्राम ।...

The Aṣṭādhyāyī of Pāṇini, edited and translated into English by Śrīśa Chandra Vasu (Allahabad: Panini office, 1891) p. 885:
"The afffix ṭhañ (+-इक) comes after the word santāpa etc. in the dative construction, in the sence of "what is able to effect that."
The word प्रभवति means 'able, capable'. The dative here has the force of अलम् (II.3.16). As संतापाय प्रभवति=सांतापिकः, साम्नाहिकः ॥

1 संताप 2 संनाह 3 संग्राम ...

5. Erroneously वाग्मिनो is printed by P. L. Vaidya

मूर्ध्नि मूर्धावसिक्तस्य दधति स्म विधानतः ॥
न त्वां प्रकृतयः सर्वाः श्रेणीमुख्याश्च भूषिताः ।
अनुव्रजितुमिच्छन्ति पौरजानपदास्तथा ॥
चतुर्भिर्वेगसम्पन्नैर्हयैः काञ्चनभूषणैः ।
मुख्यः पुष्यरथो युक्तः किं न गच्छति तेऽग्रतः ॥
न हस्ती चाग्रतः श्रीमांस्तव लक्षणपूजितः ।
प्रयाणे लक्ष्यते वीर कृष्णमेघगिरिप्रभः ॥
न च काञ्चनचित्रं ते पश्यामि प्रियदर्शन ।
भद्रासनं पुरस्कृत्य यान्तं वीर पुरस्सरम् ॥
अभिषेको यदा सज्जः किमिदानीमिदं तव ।
अपूर्वो मुखवर्णश्च न प्रहर्षश्च दृश्यते ॥[6]

"O Descendant of Raghu, the scholarly Brahmins say that today the moon is in conjunction with *Puṣya* which is the constellation of Bṛhaspati. Why do you appear sad ? your lovely face is not placed under an umbrella having a hundred ribs and white as water foam. Your face with lotuslike eyes is not fanned by two chief chowries bright as the moon or swan. O Best of Men, today the jubilant and eloquent *bandin*-s, *sūta*-s and *māgadha*-s (different kinds of bards) are not seen eulogising you with auspicious songs. The Brahmins who have completely mastered the Vedas, have not solemnly sprinkled honey and curd over your head. All the *prakṛti*-s (ministers etc.), *sreṇimukhya*-s (leaders of the guilds of traders, artisans etc.), *paura*-s (leaders of townsmen) and *jānapada*-s (leaders of country people) attired in their best do not wish to follow you. Why does the principal *puṣyaratha* not go before you, which is to be drawn by four swift horses adorned with golden ornaments ? The beautiful elephant, which is gifted with auspicious marks and resembles dark cloud and a mighty mountain, is not seen in your journey before you. O Good-looking Hero, I do not see either your servant, who must be behind the gold decorated *bhadrāsana* (royal seat), or the *bhadrāsana* itself. What has befallen you now when *abhiṣeka* ceremony is prepared? You look so unhappy that such a colour of your countenance was never seen before."

Thus, the mention of *puṣyaratha* in the *Vālmīkīya Rāmāyaṇa* along with umbrella, chowries, elephant, and *bhadrāsana* in the context of Rama's *yauvarājyābhiseka* makes it apparent that *puṣyaratha* meant a chariot to be used on the occasion of *abhiṣeka*.

In Bhāsa's *Pratimānāṭaka*, *pusyaratha* is also mentioned along with the materials which were prepared for Rāma's *yauvarājyābhiṣeka*. The passage reads as follows:

6. *Vālmīkīya Rāmāyaṇa* II. 23.8–17. [*The Vālmīki-Rāmāyaṇa* vol. II, critically edited by P. L. Vaidya (Baroda : Oriental Institute, 1962), pp. 151–152.]

प्रतिहारी– अय्य ! महाराओ देवासुरसङ्गामेसु अप्पडिहदमहारओ दसरहो आणवेदि– सिग्घं भट्टिदारअस्स रामस्स रज्जप्पंहावसञ्जोअकारआ अहिसेअसम्भारा आणीअन्तु त्ति। [आर्य, महाराजो देवासुरसङग्रामेष्वप्रति–हतमहारथो दशरथ आज्ञापयति । शीघ्रं भर्तृदारकस्य रामस्य राज्यप्रभावसंयोगकारका अभिषेकसम्भारा आनीयन्तामिति]

काञ्चुकीयः– भवति, यद् यदाज्ञप्तं महाराजेन, तत् सर्वमुपस्थापितम् । पश्य ।

छत्रं सव्यजनं सनन्दिपटहं भद्रासनं कल्पितं
न्यस्ता हेममया सदर्भकुसुमास्तीर्थाम्बुपूर्णा घटाः ।
युक्तः पुष्यरथश्च मन्त्रिसहिता : पौराः समभ्यागताः
सर्वस्यास्य हि मङ्गलं स भगवान् वेद्यां वसिष्ठः स्थितः ॥[7]

Pratīharī (personal female attendant of king) —	Sir, His Majesty King Daśaratha, who owns the irresistible great chariot in the wars between the Devas and Asuras, commands that requisite things for *abhiṣeka,* which can increase efficacy of Rāma in administration, shall be quickly brought.
Kañcukin (chamberlain)	Madam, what His Majesty commanded is all prepared. Look, umbrella, chowries, drum played on au spicious occasions and *bhadrāsana* are ready. Golden pitchers full of sacred water of holy places are also ready; in those pitchers *Kuśa* grass and different flowers are also kept. Horses are already yoked to *pusyaratha.* Ministers and leaders of townsmen also have arrived already. Vasiṣṭha, the Venerable, who is to render all these things auspicious, has already seated himself on the altar.

Thus in the *Pratimānāṭaka, Puṣyaratha* is mentioned along with other requisites for *abhiṣeka,* such as umbrella, chowrie, *bhadrāsana,* golden pitchers with water of holy places and priest. This comfirms the statement contained in the *Vālmīkīya Rāmāyaṇa* wherein *puṣyaratha* is mentioned as the royal chariot to be used during the occasion of *abhiṣeka.*

Bhaṭṭasvāmin in his *Pratipadapañcikā,* a commentary on the *Kauṭalīya Arthaśāstra,* which is partially available (i e. only from II. 8.5 to the end of the second *adhikaraṇa*), explains the above quoted *sūtra* of Kauṭalya in this way:

तद्भेदमेव तावदाह, देवरथेत्यादि । देवरथो यात्रादौ देवतासञ्चारार्थं, पुष्यरथोऽभिषेकदिवसमङ्गलादावारोहणार्थं, साङग्रामिको युद्धार्थः, पारियाणिकोऽध्वगमनार्थः, परपुराभियानिकः शत्रुदुर्गादिनियोगार्थः, वैनयिको ऽभ्यासार्थः । इत्येव षड् रथान् कारयेत्[8] ।

7. *Pratimānāṭaka* 1. 3. [*Bhāsanāṭakacakram. Plays ascribed to Bhāsa. Original Thirteen Texts in Devanāgarī,* critically edited by C.R. Devadhar (Poona : Oriental Book Agency, 1937) p. 250.]

8. "Bhaṭṭa-svāmin's Commentary on Kauṭilya's Artha-śāstra", edited by K.P. Jayaswal and A. Banerjea - Sastri, *Journal of the Bihar and Orissa Research Society*, XII (1925) p. 187.

"Kauṭalya now explains the categories of chariots. *Devaratha* means that kind of chariot used in gods' procession on festive occasions, *puṣyaratha* means that kind of chariot meant for a ride on auspicious occasions during *abhiṣeka ceremony*. *Saṅgrāmikaratha* means that kind of chariot meant for war. *Pariyānikaratha* means that kind of chariot used as a travelling coach. *Parapurābhiyānikaratha* is that kind of chariot used in the attack against enemy's fort etc. *Vainayikaratha* is that kind of chariot used during military exercises. The superintendent of chariots thus shall have six kinds of chariots made."

In the commentary of Bhaṭṭasvāmin it is clear that *puṣyaratha* is a kind of chariot used particularly on auspicious occasions of the day of *abhiṣeka*. Thus the meaning of *puṣyaratha* given by Bhaṭṭasvāmin corresponds to the implication of the *Vālmīkīya Rāmāyaṇa* and *Pratimānāṭaka*.

Inasmuch as the chariot of Red Machindra is described as *devaratha*[9] in the *thyasaphu*-s of Malla period, the explanation of Bhaṭṭasvāmin : देवरथो यात्रादौ देवतासञ्चारार्थम् (*Devaratha* means that kind of chariot used in gods' procession of festive occasions) seems in vogue in later times, too.

Let us now discuss how the royal chariot for coronation came to be known as *puṣyaratha*.

9. *The thysaphu D B* (i). [Shankar Man Rajbansi, *Aitihāsikaghaṭanāvalī* [A Document of Historical Events] (Kathmandu : Bir Library, V. S. 2020 [1963], P. 11; D. R. Regmi, *Medieval Nepal* Pt. III, pt. II [Calcutta: Firma K.L. Mukhopadhyay, 1966) p. 72]:

सं. ८०१ वैशाखशुक्लपादु भरुणीनक्षत्र शनिश्चरवार थ्व कुन्हु बुगं सारेयात देवरथस थङा दिन ॥

"Saturday, the first day of the bright half of Vaiśākha, the moon being in conjunction with the Bharaṇī asterism, the year 801. On this day *Buga* (Red Machindra) was placed on *devaratha* to be drawn";
the date is accurate and on that Saturday *Pratipad* was till 22 *ghaṭīs* and 41 *palas* and *Bharaṇī* till 34 *ghaṭīs* and 38 *palas*.

The Thyasaphu A folio 79 [D. R. Regmi, op. cit, p. 35]:

सं ८११ वैशाखशुक्ल :॥ द्वादशी हस्तनक्षत्र बुधवार ॥ थ्व कुन्हु ञलया बुगदेव गारबाहारस भेतबुतर, देव खतन कोकायाव, रथ पियाम्रो, हनों रथ चिङाम्रो देवपुत तयाम्रो देवरथस थङाम्रो यात ङायकर ॥

"Wednesday, the 12th day of the bright half of Vaiśākha, the moon being in conjunction with the Hasta asterism the year 811. On this day the chariot of Patan's *Bugadeva* (Red Machindra) was broken accidentally. The deity was removed from the *Khata* (portable shrine), the chariot was demolished, and a new one was made. Then the deity was purified and placed on *devaratha* and procession was taken out."

The date is accurate and on that Wednesday *Dvādaśī* was till 23 *ghaṭīs* and 9 *palas* and *Hasta* till 20 *ghaṭīs* and 49 *palas*.
(Both these dates at worked out by my brother Dinesh Raj Pant, co-editor of *Pūrṇimā*.)

The asterism *Puṣya* is one of the best asterisms which are prescribed by the holy texts for performance of coronation[10].

> "It is proper to perform coronation ceremony when the moon is in conjunction with *Jyeṣṭha, Śravaṇa, Āśvinī, Puṣya, Hasta, Mṛgaśiras, Citrā, Anurādhā, Revatī, Rohinī, Uttaraphālgunī, Uttarāṣādhā* or *Uttarabhādra* asterisms."

It is known from the *Vālmīkīya Rāmāyaṇa* that the *yauvarājyābhiṣeka* of Rāma was decided to be performed on the *Puṣya* asterism.[11] The *Ātharvaṇapariśiṣṭa, Bṛhatsaṁhitā, Kalikāpurāṇa* and other texts tell us that a kind of *abhiṣeka* was performed for kings on the asterism *Puṣya* and that the *abhiṣeka* was known as *Puṣyābhiṣeka*. We know from the *Gopālarājavaṁśāvalī,* the 14th century Nepalese chronicle, and other contemporary historical documents that *Puṣyā-*

10. *Vīramitrodoya Rājanītiprakāśa* [*Vīramitrodaya, Rājnīti Prakāśa by Mahāmahopādhyāya Paṇḍita Mitra Miśra,* edited by Vishnu Prasad (Benares : Chowkhamba Sanskrit Series Office, 1916) p. 58] :
सामविधानब्राह्मणेऽपि, राजानमभिषेचयेत् तिष्येन श्रवणेन वा ।

"It is written in the *Sāmavidhānabrāhmaṇa,* too.
The priest shall crown the king when the moon is in conjuction with *Puṣya* or *Śravaṇa.*"

Muhūrtacintāmaṇi X. 1–2 : [*Muhūrtacintāmaṇiḥ Pīyūṣadhārāṭīkāsametaḥ* (Muhūrtacintāmaṇi together with the Pīyūṣadhārā Commentary), edited by Govinda Śāstrī (Bombay : Śrīveṅkaṭeśvara Press, V. S. 1951 (1894), [p. 301–302] :

राजाभिषेक : शुभ :...
शाक्रश्रवक्षिप्रमृदुध्रुवोडुभि :...

Pīyūṣadhārā, [*p.* 302 *Op. cit*] :

शाक्रं ज्येष्ठा श्रवः श्रवणः क्षिप्राणि अश्विनीपुष्यहस्ता : मृदूनि मृगचित्रानुराधारेवत्यः ध्रुवाणि रोहिण्युत्तरात्रयं च एतैः उडुभि सद्भि : राजाभिषेकः शुभः ।

11. *Vālmīkīya Rāmāyaṇa* II. 4. 21–22 (*op. Cit.* p. 27):

अद्य चन्द्रोऽभ्युपगतः पुष्यात् पूर्वं पुनर्वसुम् ।
श्वः पुष्ययोगं नियतं वक्ष्यन्ते दैवचिन्तकाः ॥
तत्र पुष्येऽभिषिञ्चस्व मनस्त्वरयतीव माम् ।
श्वस्त्वाहमभिषेक्ष्यामि यौवराज्ये परंतप ॥

"Today the moon has arrived on *Punarvasu* which is immediately before *Puṣya*. Tomorrow the moon will reach *Puṣya* certainly, astrologers say so. My mind makes me hurry to perform your *abhiṣeka* in coming *Puṣya*. O Afflicter of Foes, tomorrow I will perform your *abhiṣeka* in the office of heir – apparent."

bhiṣeka was performed for some of Nepalese Kings who reigned from 1167 to 1381 and that those *puṣyābhiṣeka*-s were the inaugurations of those kings.[12]

In this context, it is worth mentioning that the coronation ceremony of King Birendra Bir Bikram Shah Dev of Nepal was solemnized on February 24th in 1975, when the moon was in conjunction with *Puṣya*. From this it is evident that the asterism *Puṣya is* very favourable as the auspicious time for coronation ceremony. It is written in the etymological explanation of the asterism *Puṣya* that the work done during this asterism becomes flourishing, so this is called *Puṣya*[13]. Therefore importance is given to *Puṣya* for the good omen. For all these reasons the royal chariot for a drive during the coronation ceremony was called *Puṣyaratha.*

12. See my "Puṣyābhiṣeka" in *Journal of Nepal Research Centre, vol. I.*

13. *Kāśikā* III. 1. 116 (*op. Cit.* pp. 202) :

पुष्यसिद्धचौ नक्षत्रे ॥११६॥

पुषेः सिधेश्चाधिकरणे क्यप् निपात्यते नक्षत्रे अभिधेये। पुष्यन्ति अस्मिन्नर्था इति पुष्यः। सिद्धचन्तिअस्मिन्निति सिद्धचः। नक्षत्रे इति किम् ? पोषणं, सेधनम्।

Śrīśa Chandra Vasu, *op. cit.* p. 392:

The words पुष्य and सिद्धच are irregularly formed by the affix क्यप्, when used as names of asterisms.
Thus पुष्+क्यप्=पुष्यः 'the Pushya asterism'. It is so called because objects are nourished under the influences of this asterism. सिध्+क्यप्=सिद्ध्यः 'the asterism Siddhya' another name of Pushya, so-called because things are accomplished under the influence of this star.
When not the names of asterisms, the forms are पोषणं 'nourishining', सेधनम् 'accomplishining'.

The Pūjāri Maṭha of the Dattātreya Temple, Bhaktapur, and its Restoration. A Preliminary Report

Heimo Rau

Bhadgaon or Bhaktapur, the smallest of the three Malla cities, is situated in the main valley of Nepal about 15 km. east of Kathmandu. According to a legend, the city was founded in 889 A. D. by Rājā ĀNANDA DEVA. Its ground-layout-plan resembles a conch, one of the emblems of Viṣṇu, and it is perched on the slope of a valley through which flows the Hanumante towards the Manohara. The temple place of the Taumadhi Tole in the west and the temple place of Dattātreya in the east are the two focal points of the city scene of Bhaktapur. They are the central points of the surrounding localities and stand out on account of their remarkable buildings. There is also the Durbar Place on the north edge of the city. Its origin lies in the decree of the rulers who built here their palace of fifty-five windows and surrounded it with all types of sanctuaries. It has nothing to do with the origin and the genuine growth of the city and still does not form a part of its daily life. The hustle and bustle of the citizens, the movements of the artisans and the traders do not touch the palace region. On the other hand, the temple places pulsate with life like the lanes of the city. From the uneven ground of the Taumadhi Tole above the five-storeyed terraces rises the five-storeyed Nyātapola Pagoda to a height of 30.48 metres[2]. This is the most impressive building of the city and was built in 1701–1702 by BHŪPATĪNDRA MALLA (1696–1721). In contrast to the steeply rising five storeys of the Pagoda tapering off, is the compact structure of the Bhairavanātha Temple situated to its east and built by JAGAJJYOTI MALLA (1614–1637)[3].

Eastward from here, at a distance of 1/2 km. and reached through bumpy brick-paved winding lanes, stands the Dattātreya Temple on a trapezium-like place

1. Names of contemporary persons and the geographical places are given in the customary transcription.

2. Exact measurement by JOSEPH SCHNEIDER.

3. The temple originally had only one storey. More storeyes were added by BHŪPATĪNDRA MALLA (1696–1721) who wanted to ensure that the older and worthier temple did not lose importance in front of the taller and younger Nyātapola Pagoda.

which is slightly sloping to the west. We have come to the older part of the city and perhaps it is here that we have to look for the centre of the first layout of the city. The Deity to whom the temple is dedicated, represents a peculiar mixture of Brahmā, Śiva and Viṣṇu. He was born as a son of Atri and Anasūyā with the blessing of these three gods. He is portrayed as a three-faced, naked ascetic dressed in tiger skin and wearing snake-earrings. He is sitting cross-legged in deep meditation and holding in his four hands a *cakra*, a *triśūla*, a *ḍamarū* and a *gadā*. He is reputed to be the teacher of Śiva and master of gods and human beings. Besides offerings of flowers, vermilion, rice, green leaves, grass, incense, camphor, perfume, curd, milk and sweets, on occasions, even bulls and goats are sacrificed to him.

The Dattātreya Temple is a three-storyed plump-looking Pagoda, and like Kāṣṭhamaṇḍapa in Kathmandu, is supposed to have been built from the wood of a single tree. This legend, as in the case of Kāṣṭhamaṇḍapa, here, too, points to the great antiquity of the holy building. The temple is mentioned for the first time under YAKṢA MALLA (1428–1482). This was at a time when the valley had not yet been divided into city states. Though many parts have been renovated, like the wood carvings, the great antiquity of the Pagoda itself is obvious, because their proportions indicate the compact, massive and closed form of the early Pagoda architecture. The Dattātreya Temple has all these distinguishing characteristics in common with the Kāṣṭhamaṇḍapa. They become particularly evident when compared with the later form of the elegant Nyātapola Pagoda.

The Dattātreya Temple is situated at a place which is the centre of life of the artisans and traders of the city of Bhaktapur. There are three temples and nine monasteries (*maṭha*) in this area. A raised platform has been built out of bricks in front of and behind the Dattātreya Temple. The temple-place narrows down and slopes slightly to the west where it adjoins the single-storyed hall of the Bhīmasena Temple (mentioned for the first time in 1654–1655). Behind it is a square-shaped water pond. The spatial relations between the three-storeyed main temple and this low hall have an impact on the place which is otherwise surrounded by low houses. One has to climb to reach the Dattātreya Temple. There is another smaller, almost square place behind the main temple which creates a sense of proportional unity as the gaps between the Pagoda and surrounding houses are narrow. On the south side of this place is situated the stately complex of the Pūjārī Maṭha belonging to the Dattātreya Temple. It leaves other *mathas* of the area far behind in size and facilities.

According to the oral tradition of the priests[4] of the Pūjārī Maṭha, this monastery was founded by GOSVĀMI GURUBAKṢA GIRI, a sādhu from Mahuragarh

4. Information about the oral traditions reproduced below and about the agreements regarding the economic management of the Pūjārī Maṭha laid down in writing and inscriptions have been communicated by RAMESH JUNG THAPA, Director of Archaeology; PURNAHARSHA BAJRACHARYA, Chief

in India who returned laden with treasure from his pilgrimage to Tibet. The Deity was solemnly enthroned in the year 606 of the Nepal era, that is in the year 1486 A. D. Friendly relations with Tibet continued for years.

The Maṭha has manifold functions:

1. It is a house of God accommodating the following Deities: Dattātreya, Viśveśvara Mahādeva, Sāmantako Mahādeva, Kālī, Gaṇeśa, Bhīmasena and the Iṣṭa Devatā Talejū, the tantric family goddess of the Mallas whose image can be seen with four heads and sixteen arms on the golden gate of the palace at the Durbar Place of Bhaktapur. The priests are obliged to perform the daily worship. The gods live on the first floor of the building. Even when the restoration work was going on, it was impossible to get a glimpse of the idols of these deities. Before dismantling and reconstruction began, the priests took them away to another place, but not without seeking, in a special *pūjā,* their forgiveness for this disturbance. After completion of the restoration work, the deities were brought back to the original place.

2. The Maṭha is the residence of the Mahanta. The first person to hold this office was the founder GURUBAKṢA GIRI. His throne is even today kept in readiness along with linen cloth, water vessel and *agnipātra* on the first floor of the house. The names of the later Mahantas are contained in a manuscript which is in the possession of KRISHNA BAHADUR GIRI. They are in chronological order as follows:

RĀMADATTA GIRI, MĀNADATTA GIRI, KIŚORA GIRI, GAUTAMA GIRI, SANTOṢA GIRI, MĀDHAVA GIRI, BALA GIRI, ŚIVA GIRI, KAILĀŚA GIRI, GUNARI GIRI, LOKANĀTHA GIRI, KULAMANA GIRI, BHŪPĀNANDA GIRI, KAILĀŚA GIRI, KĀLIKĀPRASĀDA GIRI, VIŚVĀMBHARA GIRI.

At times, the nomination of a successor took place on the death-bed when the dying Mahanta passed on the honour to his best pupil. The present Mahanta, VIŚVĀMBHARA GIRI, has renounced his rights to the priestly functions and leads the life of a *gṛhastha.* In his place, two other priests perform the *pūjā.* KṚṢṆA GIRI performs the pūjā for Sāmantako Mahādeva and for Kālī; JÑĀNI PRASĀDA for the remaining deities. This renunciation of the priestly functions and their being handed over to subordinated Brahmins makes it evident that the main duty of the Mahanta is administration. As such, he is the owner of considerable landed property and has considerable income.

Research officer; KRISHNA PRASAD SHRESTHA, Director, Bhaktapur Museum; and RAM NIWAS PANDEY, Lecturer, Department of Nepalese History, Culture and Archaeology, Tribhuvan University. Thanks are due to them for their suggestions important enough to lead to more through examination of the subject.

Ill 1, 2 *The Pūjārī Maṭha before and after restoration*

He has to give from this a sum of 500 rupees yearly to the Guṭhī Saṁsthān which represents a higher administrative council for religious charities. Guṭhī Saṁsthān has considerable funds at its disposal and has also contributed a large sum towards the restoration of the Pūjārī Matha. From these incomes, the Mahanta has not only to equip the Dattātreya Temple and its Maṭha with items required for regular *pūjā* but also a number of other temples. The Mahanta of the Pūjārī Maṭha has to incur particularly heavy expenses during major festivals. He has to arrange for the boarding and lodging of the hordes of pilgrims and the firewood which keeps them warm in winter. The Maṭha has provided for them large dormitories.

3. A further function of the Maṭha, at least in the past, was to look after theological studies. It not only offered boarding and lodging to its permanent residents and pilgrims, but also provided medical help whenever necessary. According to tradition, even the study of Indian and Tibetan medicine was undertaken.

The house as it stands today differs greatly from the original built in the fifteenth century. An earthquake during the reign of VIŚVA MALLA (1548–1560) damaged the building so badly that it had to be reconstructed. Tradition has it that extensive repair work was undertaken when KRIPĀLA GIRI and LOKANĀTHA GIRI were Mahantas. This must have been the architectural construction and design of woodwork which gave the Maṭha its present appearance. If we go down the line of the Mahantas and if we roughly estimate four to five Mahantas per century, we can place LOKANĀTHA GIRI in the nineteenth and KRIPĀLA GIRI in the eighteenth century. So, it is evident from these traditions that in every century a thorough renovation of the existing structure was necessary. Both the stone inscriptions installed in 1763 in the middle courtyard (B) of the Matha during the reign of the last Malla king of Bhaktapur, refer to the restoration being done in the eighteenth century. The earthquake of 1934 came when KAILĀŚAPRASĀDA was the Mahanta. It caused extensive damage in the whole of Nepal and destroyed a number of important monuments completely. The walls of the Maṭha came out of plumb and the normal drainage was blocked with the result that dampness affected the walls and the woodwork. The bricks and wood connections closely linked to each other were squeezed out of shape. The worst damaged parts were repaired out of necessity. However, for decades the condition remained critical.

The four-storeyed Maṭha, with a perimeter of about 34 metres in the north-south direction and 23 metres in the east-west direction and a height of 11 metres (only the towerlike Pagoda roof rises to a height of 15 metres), is arranged around three courtyards. Courtyard A is the smallest, containing a wall now dry and out of use. The wood-carved window frames had fallen down. In contrast, Courtyard B offered a breathtaking view. Rich windows were preserved on all four sides right up to the roof. It was a matter of grave concern that in this courtyard a public well had been installed which caused permanent damp-

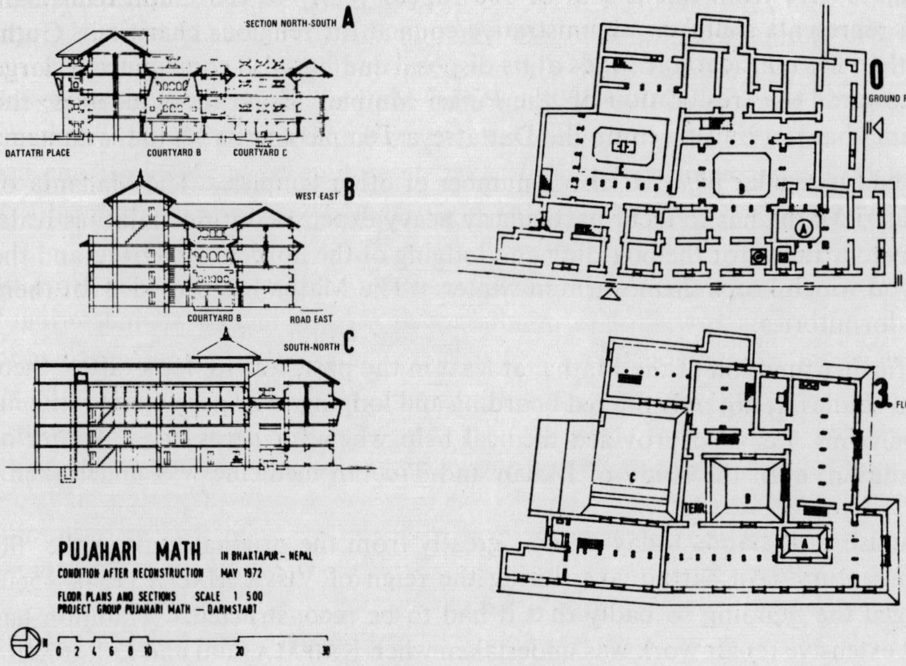

Ill. 3 *Floor plans and map of the surrounding area*

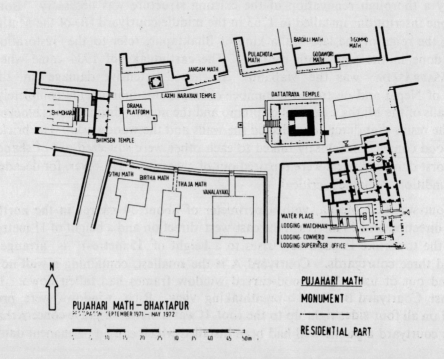

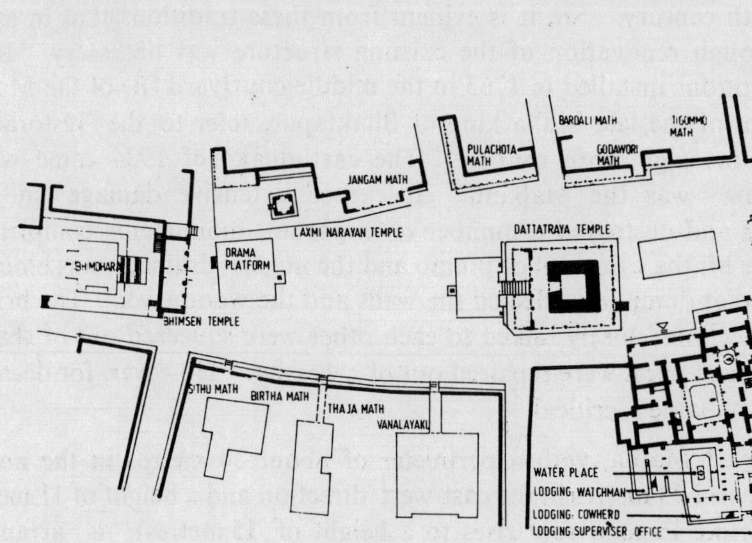

ness and posed a grave danger to the wood carvings. Courtyard C like Courtyard A was completely destroyed; the windows had disappeared; the walls partly collapsed. Cows roamed there which made it look like a stockyard fallen into disrepair. The roofs of the whole building complex had holes in many places; the walls were out of plumb and riddled with cracks. In addition to the damages caused by the earthquake of 1934, further decay had taken place. If one had seen the magnificent building in that condition, one would not have thought that it would survive another monsoon.

The wood carvings enhance the special charm of the Maṭha. A view from the roof down the narrow, square middle courtyard (B) reveals an indescribable abundance of ornamental forms and figures which are woven into each other in a close weave. The windows, not only in the courtyards but also on the north façade of the house, look like oriel balconies. They have benches inside which are comfortable to sit on and from where one, while leaning on the balustrade, can steal a glance of the street. The east side of the building which runs along a narrow lane, is decorated with different types of peacock windows. The best preserved window shows the body of the bird in the centre and the spread out feathers serve as a filling for the circular opening of the window. The superb execution of the motif has greatly contributed towards the fame of this artistic monument. Besides the rich windows which decorate the façades and the middle courtyard (B), the carvings of the low main door on the north side of the Maṭha display a perfection in the art of ornamental and figure carving.

Ill. 4 *Main door on the Northern side*

Ill. 5 *The peacock window*

The door frame, richly decorated with redoubled lines, has in its centre a tiny Śiva seated on a throne. Its lintel is elongated. From above the Śiva, Garuḍa looks down on those who are entering. He is holding in his claws two Nāgas who appear to immediately flow in opposite directions in endless coils. Below in a sunken flat relief, there are, in a line between the sun an the moon, eight auspicious signs. The very ancient motif of *yakṣīs* guarding on both sides of the door has been replaced by the river goddesses who swing out in the traditional way on the right and the left. The two goddesses are standing on the jaws of a *makara*. Here, though the tortoise is missing, the goddesses are meant to be Gaṅgā and Yamunā, who are seen with their respective distinguishing *vahanas* on the windows of the inner courtyard, too. In the top wedge near the door frame on both sides, a four-armed Viṣṇu is shown sitting, while at the foot of the frame, eight-armed Bhairavas are frightening away the demons.

These carvings originated from one of the best workshops of Bhakatapur which must have flourished under the last two Malla rulers who were connoisseurs of art. They give us a conception of a branch of art which is rarely preserved in India.

The Nepal Government had requested the German Government in the middle sixties to have some historically and artistically important buildings in the valley of Nepal restored by German experts. The author of this report was commissioned by the Ministry of Foreign Affairs and could only survey the monuments in question in 1969. He selected, in agreement with the Archaeological Department of Nepal, the Pūjārī Maṭha of the Dattātreya Temple and suggested to

Ill. 6 *Restoration work in full swing*

the German Government that it was worth restoring[5]. In the following year, the President of the Federal Republic of Germany formally presented the means to restore this monument as the German Government's wedding present to H. H. the then CROWN PRINCE BIRENDRA.

However, the actual restoration campaign started only when the author won a group of four architects of the Technical University Darmstadt for his assistance. They were GERHARD AUER, HANS BUSCH, NIELS GUTSCHOW and WILFRIED KROEGER. They worked under the joint responsibility of RAMESH JUNG THAPA and HEIMO RAU and were assisted from the Nepal side by KRISHNA PRASAD SHRESTHA, PURNAHARSHA BAJRACHARYA, PUSHPA PRASAD LUINTEL and many others. So the work could be completed as scheduled within eight months, from September 1971 to May 1972.

5. Vide report in Jahrbuch des Südasien-Instituts der Universität Heidelberg, Vol. III, 1968–1969. 136 ff. and pp. of this book.

Ill. 7 *Wood-carvers working at a new window*

The restoration did not aim at renovation. Wall after wall was examined and only when found completely unserviceable, broken down and rebuilt. Old material was used as far as possible and the use of new bricks was limited to the unimportant parts of the building and which were not easily visible. The aim was to avoid the new construction becoming conspicuous in front of the old surroundings. Courtyard C, the worst damaged, was built anew and had its windows replaced from other buildings of the city. The living quarters are in the East, West and the South wings of this courtyard, the space for workshops is on the ground floor and on the first floor there are large halls for accommodating pilgrims. The public well situated in Courtyard B was transferred to Courtyard C. Thus, independent of the older arrangement, Courtyard C was purposely rebuilt as a residential area with boarding facilities. Care was taken that the whole structure remained homogeneous and did not upset daily life and was not out of place on the social context of the city. Just this fact enabled us to insulate the well preserved Courtyard B and its wings from all damaging influences. Daily life and activity could continue in and around Courtyard C. *Pūjā,* with all its paraphernalia, should concentrate on Courtyard B, the original character of which in all its details can now be preserved without outside interference. The fact that it is open to visitors should not hinder its preservation. Its floors will house various collections. There is a particular plan to have here a Museum of religious antiques. The preservation of the woodwork was the main anxiety of the Archaeological Department of Nepal. With the help of the Wuerttemberg State Museum in Stuttgart[6], wood samples of the Nepalese buildings were examined and their sensitivity to insect damage investigated. Bayer's Xylamon Tr was recommended both for treatment against decay and pests. Every single girder in the Pūjārī Maṭha was treated with the preserving substance either by dipping or by spraying, especially the woodcarvings. These were first dismantled and then cleaned individually. Missing parts were replaced only when absolutely necessary and in such a way that the replacement remained easily detectable. It was found that the local wood carvers could copy the ornamental parts but had difficulties to carve out the figures. As old bricks were in short supply, experiments were conducted successfully to make new bricks by firing them according to the old formula. There were about 150 workers including masons, carpenters and carvers employed at a time. There was also a small team of experts engaged in the chemical preservation of the wood. The help of Nepalese colleagues was very necessary and definitely contributed to the success of the project. Thus the first Nepal-German restoration campaign was successfully concluded. It left behind not only the Pūjārī Maṭha, which will for a few decades defy any monsoon storm, but also a team of well-trained technicians who will be available for future projects of a similar kind. It has now been followed by the Bhaktapur Town Developing Project which is using the Pūjārī Maṭha as its headquarters and office premises.

6. Thanks are due to HILMAR SCHICKLER and his colleagues at the Landesmuseum Stuttgart for their friendly assistance.

Ill. 8, 9 *H.M. KING BIRENDRA's visit to the restoration site. Mr. R. J. Thapa, Director of the Dpt. of Archeology, left, Prof. Dr. H. Rau right of His Majesty.*

In conclusion it should be mentioned that H. M. KING BIRENDRA took keen interest in the restoration work. He asked for continuous reports on the progress made and came himself to visit the site on 2nd November 1971. When the whole work was completed Her Majesty QUEEN AISHWARYA graciously accepted the key of the building on 28th June, 1972.

Three Unpublished Inscriptions Concerning the Devabhājus of Patan

Aishvarya Dhar Sharma

In this paper I publish three hitherto unpublished inscriptions of the Malla period which provide us with some information about the Devabhāju Brahmins of Patan.

The Devabhājus bear the Sanskrit appellation *Rājopādhyāya,* which means the preceptor of the king. Being preceptors of the Malla kings of the Kathmandu Valley, they are known by this appellation. Even now the Devabhājus officiate in the social and religious ceremonies of the Śaivite Newars.

The population of the Devabhājus is too small in comparision with that of their *yajamānas.* The Devabhājus have scarcely 100 families in the three cities of the Kathmandu Valley.

No. 1.

There is the temple of Pūrṇacaṇḍī in the south of Ga Bahal. Outside the temple is a big tank locally known as *Puñcalī Pukhu* (the tank of Pūrṇacaṇḍī). In front of the tank is a ruinous old *pāṭī* where the slab of stone is set on the wall facing east. The text is in Sanskrit and Newari and the script employed is Newari. At the top of the slab before the text begins a *śivaliṅga* with a hooded serpent is carved. In the upper part of the *liṅga* Candra and Sūrya are carved and in the right and left sides of that Bhṛṅgin and Nandin are inscribed respectively. The size of the slab is 44.5 × 32 in centimetre. The date is N. S. 836.

In the first verse Śaṅkara and Bhavānī are envoked. The second verse describes Vaṁśīdhara Śarmā, the son of Harihara Śarmā. He is described as the reciter of the Vedas, *agnihotrin* and scholar of *kāvyaśāstra.* The last verse tells us that Vaṁśīdhara consecrated the image of Śaṅkara and Bhavānī on Thursday, 14th day of the bright half of Māgha, in N. S. 836.

१. १ ॐ नमः श्री भवानीशङ्कराभ्यां ।। मृगपतिवृषभाङ्कौ भुक्तिमुक्तिप्रदत्तौ त्रि–
२. दशदितिजपूज्यौ निष्कलंकाङ्गदोषौ । अखिलभुवननाथौ भक्तिहृत्पूर्ण्ण–
३. कुम्भौ ॱ कृतकलुषविनाशौ तौ भजाम्यऽद्रिजेशौ ।। ।। विप्रो वंशीधरोऽसौ हरि–
४. हरतनयस्सत्यवादी सुधीमान् ॱ विध्युक्तव्यक्तिवेदध्वनिहतदुरितस्सा–
५. धुलोकप्रसंगः । ब्रह्मध्यानैकचित्त ॱ ष्प्रथितगुणपटुष्काव्यशास्त्रार्थविज्ञ–
६. स्तेजो धौम्यर्षितुल्यो द्विजकुलतिलको भासते स्माऽग्निहोत्रः ।। ।। रसा ऽ–
७. नलेभे तपसा वलक्षे ॱ तिथौ गिरीशस्य गुरौ दिनेऽस्मिन् ॱ तयोष्प्रतिष्ठां कुरुते स्म भ–
८. क्त्या जनाश्रयेऽत्यन्तमनोहरे सः ।। ।। अतः परं देशभाखा लिख्यते ।। ।। श्रेयोऽ
९. स्तु संवत् ८३६ माघशुक्लचतुर्द्दशी पुष्यानक्षत्रे ॱ आयुष्मानयोगे ॱ बृहस्पतिवासरे
१०. थ्व कुन्हु वंलानिह्मया द्विजवर अग्निहोत्र श्रीवंशीधल देवशर्माण ॱ स्वपत्नी ली–
११. लावती ब्राह्मणी स्त्रीपुरुषसन ॱ वंलापुखुलिसि वंतास थव अजाजु श्रीजर्यास–
१२. हदेवन ह्ङवस दयकं तया फले जीर्ण्णोद्धार याङाओ श्री ३ भवानीशङ्करमूर्त्ति
१३. प्रतिष्ठा यास्यं स्थापना याङा दिन जुलो ।। ।। पुनर्भाखा वर्षबन्धनस देवपूजा याय–
१४. माल ॱ जु १ पूजाभंडिल ॱ पंचामृत ॱ धूप ॱ दीप ॱ निशराव जु १ प्रोहितयात ।। जाके
१५. फं १ ।। पूर्ण्णिमा पति पूजा यायमाल ।। पूर्ण्णचण्डिस वर्षबंधन कुन्हु पूजा याय–
१६. माल ।। गाडबाहालयात्रास ज्यावलयातस ॱ पूर्ण्णचण्डीया ॱ यात्रास थ्व स्व यातसं मत ५ चछोयके–
१७. माल पूर्ण्णचण्डीया ॱ यात्रास दान बियमाल ॱ फं २ सियाबजि ॱ रा कुड १ म्वात प्र २ पालु प्र
१८. १ ॱ धलिपात ४ ॱ कुड २ बजिवाले थ्वते दान बियमाल ।। थ्वतेया साक्षी स्वपुत्र श्रीमु–
१९. ररीधर ॱ स्वगोत्र श्रीगंगानन्दन ॱ श्रीलक्ष्मीनन्दन ॱ श्रीशिवनन्दन ॱ थ्वते दृष्ट–
२०. साक्षी जुलो ।। थ्व फले ॱ देव ॱ ल्वह्रो ॱ सुनान स्यनकलसा पञ्चमहापातक
२१. लाक जुलो ॱ सुनानं निदान या–
२२. तसा उत्तरोत्तर जु–
२३. लो ।। शुभमस्तु ।।

बु रो २ पुराण खोल थ्वया वलशाणन
बुसाधं मत चछोयके । स्यह्लोयात नपं
जुरो ।। सेवक रत्नराज स्त्रीपुरुष ।।

Translation of the Newari Portion

Let it be auspicious.

On Thursday, Āyuṣmān Yoga, Puṣya Nakṣatra, the fourteenth day of the bright half of the month of Māgha in the year 836. ŚrīVaṁśīdhara Devaśarmā, an *agnihotrin* Brahmin living in the locality called Vamlānimha, along with his wife Līlāvatī Brāhmaṇī, repaired the *Phale* on the eastern side of the tank called Vamlāpukhuli built by his late grandfather ŚrīJayasiṁhadeva and also consecrated an idol of ŚrīBhavānī-Śaṅkara.

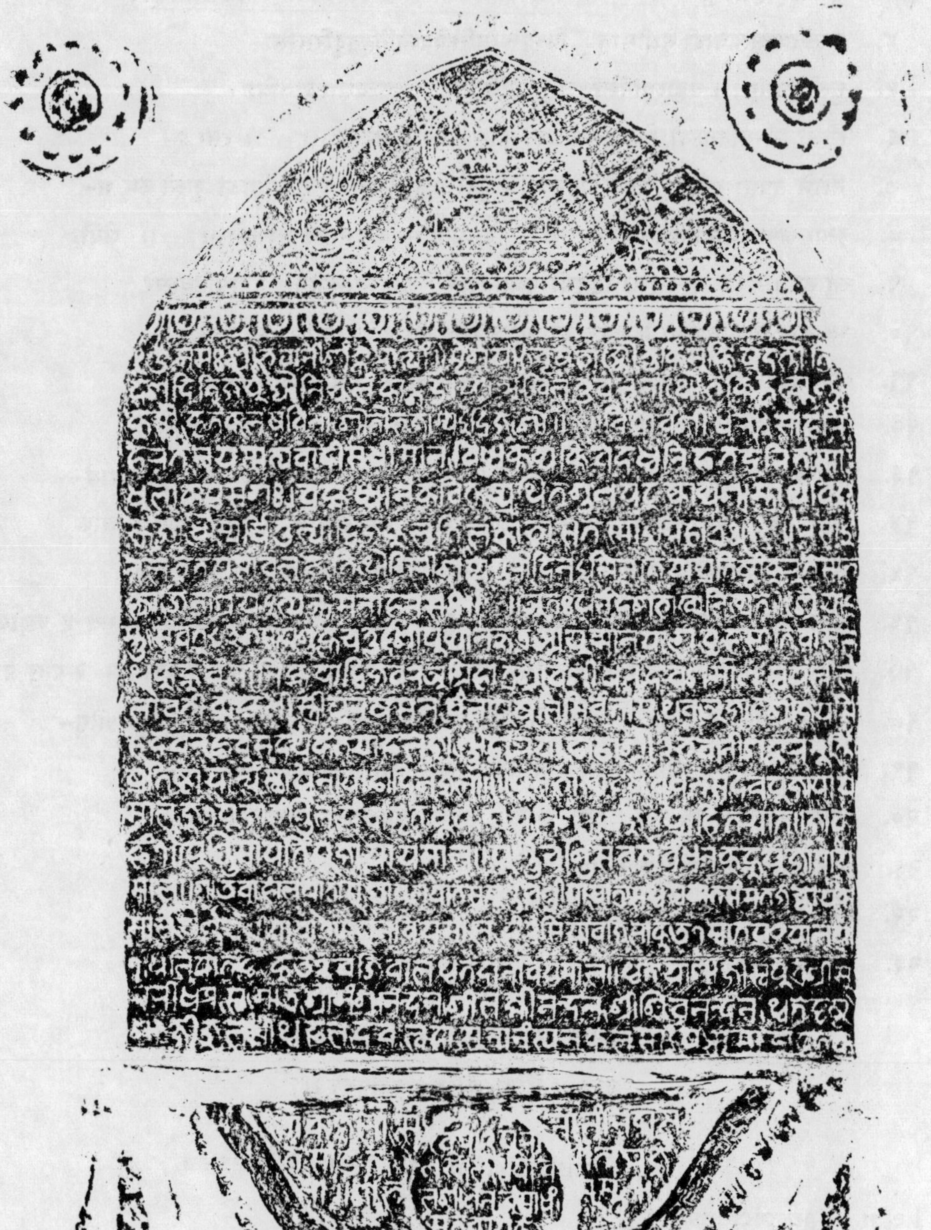

Inscr. No. 1

Again in the local language :

On the anniversary day one has to observe the worship of the deity with one set of *pūjā* offerings with *pañcāmṛta,* incense and lights and has to give in charity one set of *niśarāva* (a plate of beaten rice with confection in the form of bread) and $1^1/_2$ *pāthī* measure of rice to the priest. The deity has to be worshiped every full moon day. On the anniversary day, the goddess Pūrṇacaṇḍī has to be worshipped and on other three occasions, i. e. on the day of [chariot] festival [of Matsyendranātha] in Gāḍabāhāla, on the day of [chariot] festival [of Matsyendranātha] in Jyāvala and also on the day of the festival of Pūrṇacaṇḍī, one has to burn lights. On the day of the festival of Pūrṇacaṇḍī, the following materials are to be given in charity, viz. two pāthi measure of popped rice called *Siyābaji,* one *kuḍa* full of meat, two *pra* measure of soyabean, one *pra* measure of ginger, four potfuls of curd and two *kuda* of beaten rice both mixed.

Witnesses for this are the following— His own son Muralīdhara. Śrī Gaṅgānandana, ŚrīLakṣmīnandana, ŚrīŚivanandana all of his own gotra.
In case somebody does harm to the *phale,* the image of the deity and the stone paved he will incur the five kinds of heinous sins. On the other hand if anybody will take care of these he will have prosperity.
Let it be auspicious.

With the income of the two ropanis of land called Purāṇa Khola one should burn lights on the anniversary day, and also should do the necessary repair work. Ratnarāja and his wife are to be the care-takers.

No. 2.

The slab of stone is now lying on the ground floor of a private house in a quadrangle of Mahādeva Nani, Vala Tole, Ga Bahal. The text is in Sanskrit and Newari and the script employed is Newari. At the top of the slab before the text begins *Veṇudhara* Kṛṣṇa is carved in *Tribhaṅga* posture. The size of the slab is 48 X 33 in centimetre. The date is N. S. 866.

In the first verse Kṛṣṇa is envoked. The second verse describes Harivaṁśa Śarmā[1] belonging to Garga Gotra. He is described as a great poet and scholar of *vyākaraṇa, kośa, sāhitya, purāṇa* and other śāstras. The third verse is devoted to the description of Rājaguru Parśurāma Śarmā who was the son of Harivaṁśa

[1] A Newari–Sanskrit wordbook in verse by Harivaṁśa Sarmā is being edited by Thakurlal Manandhar and will soon be published by the Nepal Research Centre.

Sarmā. He was proficient in dance. In the fourth verse Parśurāma's son Cakrapāṇi Śarmā is described. He was scholar of *nāṭyaśāstra* and devotee of Viṣṇu. The fifth verse describes Cakrapāṇi's wife Lakṣmī and their daughter Kuleśvarā. The last two verses tell us that Cakrapāṇi consecrated the image of Kṛṣṇa and a *jaladroṇī* (water spout) with the golden tap, on Wednesday, 5th day of the bright half of Jyeṣṭha, in N. S. 866 when *ayutāhuti* (The offering of ten thousand homa) was performed and distribution of cloth and money was made.

१. ॐ श्रीकृष्णाय नम: ।। सत्त्राणदुष्टगणनाशतनूप्रसूतं ् यो-
२. गीसमाहितसमाधिपथानुगम्यं । गोपीमुखांबुजलस-
३. द्भ्रममाणभृंगं ् कृष्णं नमामि महिमाकलितं त्रिलोकं ।।
४. गर्ग्गान्वयेभूद्धरिवंशशर्म्मा दयार्द्र शीलः किल साधु-
५. रासीत् । महाकविर्व्याकरणादिकोष ् साहित्यशास्त्रादि-
६. पुराणविज्ञः ।। तस्यात्मजोभूद्द्विजपर्शुरामः ख्यातः पृ-
७. थिव्यामिव नृत्यनाथः । विचक्षणो राजगुरुर्गुणाढ्यः स्व-
८. धर्म्ममार्ग्गानुगतस्वभावः ।। श्रीचक्रपाणिस्तनयोथ
९. तस्य ् बभूव नानानटशास्त्रविज्ञः । स्वकर्म्मधर्म्मवृतपुण्य-
१०. युक्तो ् भक्त्यार्च्चितो विष्णुपदारविन्दे ।। तस्य पुण्यवती प-
११. त्नी ् धर्म्मकारी पतिवृता । नाम्ना लक्ष्मी समाख्याता ् त-
१२. त्पुत्री सा कुलेश्वरा ।। संवत्सरे स्कन्दरसेभयाते ् ज्ये-
१३. ष्टे सिते नागतिथौ बुधेस्मिन् । हुत्वायुतैराहुतिसद्वि-
१४. धानैः जनाश्रयेत्यन्तमनोभिरामे ।। सुवर्ण्णचूडे जलधे-
१५. नुयुक्ते ् दत्तेन वस्त्राण्यपि दक्षिणाभिः । कृष्णस्य मूर्त्ते
१६. जगदीश्वरस्य ् ह्यकारि तेन प्रतिमा प्रतिष्ठा ।। ।।
१७. अतः परं नेपालभाषा ।। सं ८६६ ज्येष्ठमासे शुक्ल-
१८. पक्षे पंचम्यां तिथौ पुष्यनक्षत्रे वृद्धियोगे बुद्ध-
१९. वासरे ् एतस्मिन्दिने ओरानिह्मतोरया
२०. पर्शुरामपुत्र श्रीचक्रपाणिशर्म्मणसन गा-
२१. दबाहारतोरस सतर धर्म्मशारा दय-
२२. कं अहोरात्र यज्ञ यास्यं श्री ३ कृष्ण-
२३. मूर्त्ति दयकं प्रतिष्ठा याङा दिन शुभ ।

Translation of the Newari Portion

On Wednesday, Vṛddhi Yoga, Puṣya Nakṣatra, the fifth day of the bright half of the month of Jyeṣṭha in the year 866, Cakrapāṇi Śarmā, the son of Parśurāma living in the locality called Oṃrānimha Tora consecrated an idol of Kṛṣṇa and a *dharmaśālā* at Gādabāhāra Tora by performing a yajña, for a day and a night.
Let it be auspicious.

Inscr. No. 2

No. 3.

There is a tank locally known as Taḥ Pukhu (big tank) which is to the east of Jawala Khel and to the west of Lagan Khel. To the south of the tank there is a ruinous old *Pāṭī* where the slab of stone facing east is set on the wall. The text is in Sanskrit and Newari and the script employed is Newari. At the top of the slab an image of Umā–Maheśvara is embossed. The size of the slab is 40.5 X 31.5 in centimetre. The date is N. S. 876.

In the first and second verses Viṣṇu and Śiva are envoked respectively. The third and fourth verses tell us that Ratnadhara Śarmā together with his wife Candralakṣmī, his daughter's son Mahādeva and Mahādeva's wife Rudrāṇī consecrated the image of Viṣṇu and a *dharmaśālā* on the 10th day of the dark half of Jyeṣṭha when the moon was in conjunction with the asterism Aśvinī in N. S. 876.

१. श्री ३ शंकराय नमः ।।

२. स्तुवन्ति ब्रह्मादित्रिदशनिवहा यं मधुरिपुं प्रसन्नाकारं वै कलुषकरिकण्ठीरव–

३. मिव । त्रिलोकानां भीतिप्रशमितमहद्धेतुमसकृत्तमीडे गोविन्दं जलधितनयाका–

४. न्तमजिते ।। ।। येनामर्षविलोकितेन निहतो भालेक्षणेनात्मभूर्य्यस्या केन

५. गजा स्थिता सह तया क्रीडन्तमीषत्स्मितं । गङ्गार्द्धेन्द्रयुतोत्तमाङ्गविकटं दर्व्वीकराल–

६. कृतं शश्वद् ब्रह्मविदो स्मरन्ति गिरिशं यं शङ्करन्तं भजे ।।

७. आसीच्छ्रीरत्ननामा द्विजकुलमलिनाहर्प्पतिः सत्यवादी ् तत्पत्नी चन्द्रलक्ष्मी नमि–

८. तगुणयुता भर्तृसेवातिदक्षा । तस्या दौहित्र एको ह्यभवदपि महादेवनामा दया–

९. लू ् रुद्राणी तस्य पत्नी सुकृतमतिमती दानशीला च साध्वी ।।

१०. अब्दे रसाशेभयुते दशम्यां शुचावशुक्ले खलु दस्रभेऽस्मिन् । पीताम्बरेणान्वितध–

११. र्म्मशालां चकार तां रत्नधरः सुरम्यां ।। अतः परं नेपालभाषा ् श्रेयोऽस्तु संवत् ८७६

१२. ज्येष्ठमासे कृष्णपक्षे दशम्यां तिथौ अशिनीनक्षत्रे अतिगन्धयोगे बृहस्पतिवासरे थ्व

१३. कुन्हु वलानिह्मम‌हादेवननिवन्तागृहस्थद्विजवरश्रीरत्नधरशर्म्मणा श्रीलक्ष्मीनारायण–

१४. मूर्त्ति श्रीउमामहेश्वरमूर्तिसहित थ्व धर्म्मशाला प्रतिष्ठा याना जुरो ।। थ्वते देवनित्य–

१५. पूजागुथि नामन बु दुन्ता ।। रोप २ मसिसा बायमतेव बु रोप २ नसिजह्ल थथुप बु कर्ष १ च्छी

१६. ह्लायख्वात बु थ्वते ङापिक बुया वलसानन नित्यपूजा याक ब्राह्मणयात फं २५ जाकि

१७. वर्षप्रति बियमाल ।। लग्नयात कुन्हु फं १ चेकनया मत च्छोयके जु २ निश्राव दं ४ दक्षिणा प–

१८. ञ्चामृत दयकं देवपूजा यायमाल ।। फं १ सियाबजि सह्मय जोलनसहित फं १ बजि धौलि–

१९. न वालाव दान बियमाल ।। थ्वतेया चिन्ता याक गोष्ठी षालाच्छेदैवज्ञ शिवनन्द भा–

२०. रो महापालदैवज्ञ महादेव भारो थ्वतेसन वर्षप्रति अविच्छिन्न याङ चिन्ता यायमाल जुरो फरे प्व–

२१. षु ह्लोने मार फरे रिवने बु रो १ रोभानि पापानि यातसा पञ्चमहापातक रायुव शुभमस्तु

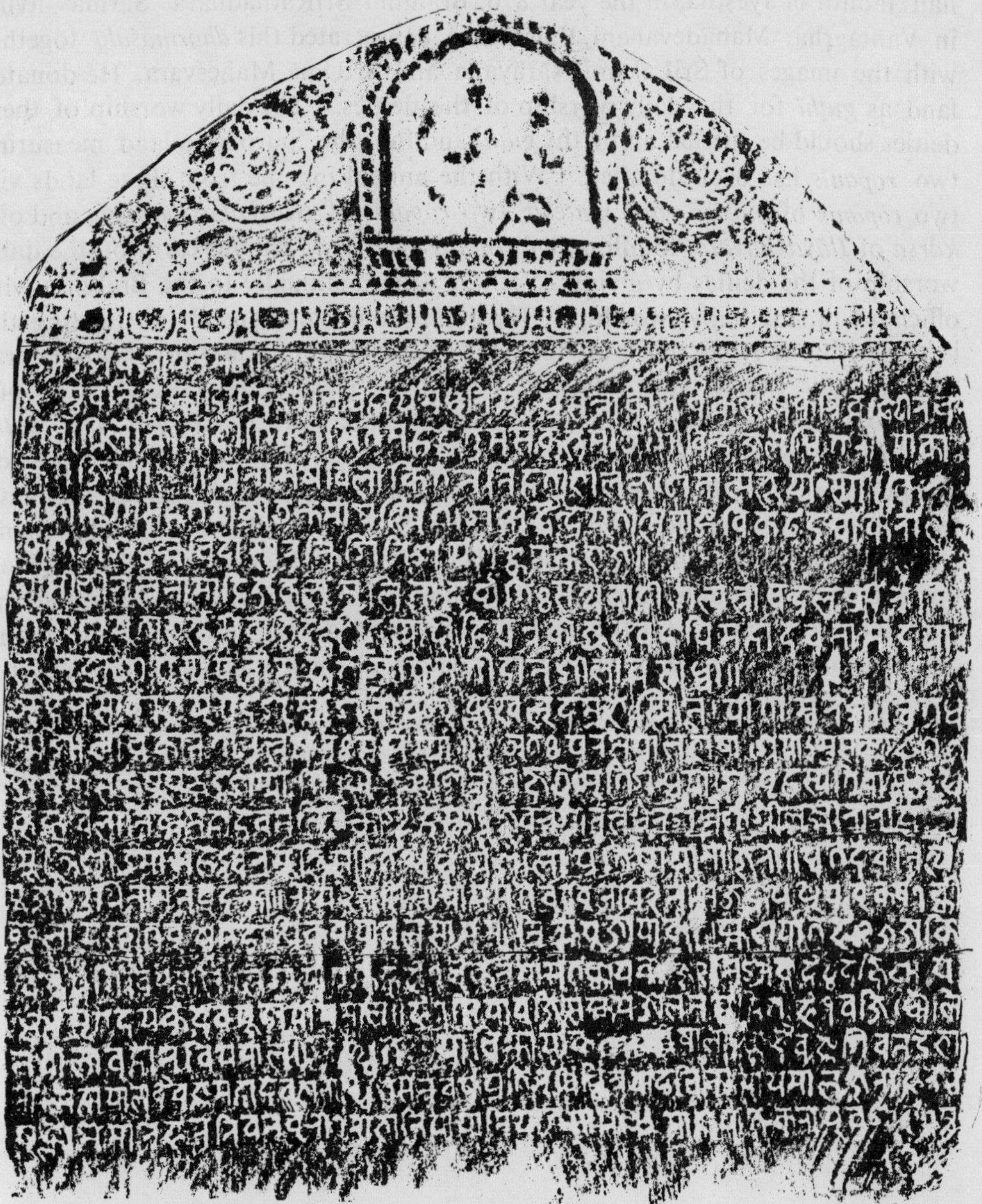

Inscr. No. 3

Translation of the Newari Portion

Let it be auspicious.

on Thursday, Atiganda yoga, Aśvinī Nakṣatra, the fourteenth day of the dark half month of Jyeṣṭha, in the year 876. Brahmin ŚrīRatnadhara Śarmā living in Vantagṛha, Mahādevanani, Valānihma, consecrated this *dharmaśālā* together with the images of ŚrīLakṣmī-Nārāyaṇa and ŚrīUmā-Maheśvara. He donated land as *guṭhī* for the daily worship of the deities. The daily worship of these deities should be carried on by the *guṭhī* and for the purpose a land measuring two *ropanis* has been donated. With the annual income from these lands viz. two *ropanis* of *masisā vāya mateva*, two *ropanis* of *Nasijalha thathupa* and one *karṣa* of *Ilāyakhavāta,* totalling five ropanis, the *guṭhī* should carry on the daily worship of the deities by giving 25 *pāthīs* of rice annually to the Brahmin who officiates in the daily worship. The *guṭhī* should also spend in lighting the lamps with one *pāthī* of oil on the day of festival of [Chariot] Matsyendra-nātha in Lagna two sets of *Niśrāva,* cash amounting to four *dammas* as *dakṣinā* and worship the deities together with *Pañcāmṛta.* The *guṭhī* should also distribute in charity one *pāthī* of beaten rice together with roasted and puffed rice (*siyābaji*) mixed with curd. The members of this *guṭhī* who have to look into this business are:— Daivajña Śivānanda Bhāro of Khālacchem, Daivajña Mahādeva Bhāro of Mahāpāla. They should look after this work all through the year uninterruptedly. They should also repair the *phale* and also the tank and should not covet the land lying behind the *phale* measuring one ropani donated for the purpose. If they do they will incur the five kinds of heinous sins. Let it be auspicious.

An Unknown Upaniṣad of the Kṛṣṇa Yajurveda: The Kaṭha-Śikṣā-Upaniṣad

Michael Witzel

1. Among the Upaniṣads of the Black Yajurveda, it is the Kathopaniṣad (KU) that holds a special position: among the Hindus it is held in highest esteem, and in the West, too, it is one of the Upaniṣads read most frequently, because of the important position it holds in Hindu thought.

The short prose legend (KU I 1–6) preceding the main portion of this Upaniṣad, i.e. the versified dialogue of Yama and Naciketas, is identical almost word by word with the Naciketas legend of another school of the Yajurveda, i.e. the one contained in Taittirīya – Brāhmaṇa (TB) III 11, 8. This is well-known since WEBER[1] and v. DEUSSEN.[2] Yet, in spite of WEBER's, v. DEUSSEN's, and especially also v. SCHROEDER's articles,[3] not enough attention has been paid to the fact that this portion of the TB (as well as all its concluding ones and the beginning of the Taittirīya – Āraṇyaka (TĀ) did not belong originally to the 'canonical' texts of the Taittirīyas but have been taken over word by word[4] from the lost

1) WEBER, Literaturgeschichte, passim (cf. p. 98 sqq.)

2) v. DEUSSEN, Sechzig Upaniṣads des Veda, repr. Darmstadt, 1963, p. 262

3) v. SCHRÖDER, Die Tübinger Kaṭha – Handschriften und ihre Beziehung zum Taittirīya– Āraṇyaka, Vienna 1889 (Sitzungsberichte der Kaiserlichen Akademie der Wissenschaften, phil.-hist. Klasse, Bd. *CXXXVII*) p. 6 sq.; cf. also RENOU, Écoles védiques p. 146, 174, 177, 179; N. TSUJI, Genzon Yajurveda Bunken (Existent Yajurveda Literature), Tōyō Bunko Ronsō, Ser. A Vol. LII, Tōkyō 1970 p. 52, 134 with annotation 488, 490; CALAND, in his German translation of the Āpastamba-Śrautasūtra: introduction to XLX 11, (Vol. III p. 183), and present author, in the edition of Kaṭha-Āraṇyaka, introduction, annotation 7, = (Nepal Research Centre Publications, vol. 2, Wiesbaden 1976).

Now RAGHU VĪRA's fragmentary Ms. of the (Kapiṣṭhala) Kaṭha-Brāhmaṇa, corresponding to TB III 12, has to be added, see ed. of KapS., repr. Delhi 1968 p. XIX sq.

4) and with all the phonetical peculiarities of the Kaṭhas, like *svàr* (K) instead of *súvar* (T).

Katha–Brahmana (KaṭhB, only fragments of which remain), although this fact is not unknown to Hindu tradition.[5]

The Naciketas legend of the Kaṭha-Śākhā thus preserved in the TB, in fact, has to be assigned to the late Brāhmaṇa/Āraṇyaka period because of the central role played in this legend by the problem of the gradual diminishing of the effects of the rituals (*iṣṭapūrta–*), the 'dying again' (*punarmṛtyu*) caused by it, and the wish to 'conquer this second death' (*punarmṛtyum... apa han–*). This short legend, therefore, has to be regarded as a fragment of early Upaniṣadic thought of the Kaṭha School, preserved only through lucky coincidence.

This characterisation of the Kaṭha's Naciketas legend preserved in the TB is also warranted by the use of the perfect [6] as the tense of narration, a fact not known from other Kaṭha texts (which still use the imperfect); perfect tense in narration is clearly a sign of late composition in the texts of this *śākhā*. The version of the Naciketas story preserved in the Kaṭhopaniṣad, however, is a still later[7] redaction of the traditional legend, as it has already been composed in verses and as it also is more developed in its philosophical contents. Yet it still attaches itself to the old narrational tradition, in repeating the beginning prose phrases from the KaṭhB (and TB).

As this versified form of the Kaṭhopaniṣad known to us is already counted among the second layer of Upaniṣadic texts, the Kaṭha School, therefore, seemingly cannot claim any old Upaniṣadic text like those represented by the Bṛhadāraṇyaka-Up., Chāndogya-Up., or even the Taittirīya-Up. (TU).

2. In the so called *Ṛcakas*[8] of the Kashmirian Paṇḍits, however, whose Śākhā is the Kaṭha- School of the Black Yajurveda, there is to be found an *aupaniṣada–vrata*[9], i.e. one of the special observances to be followed when

5) designated as: *aṣṭau kāṭhakāni*, see e.g. SĀYAṆA's introduction to TĀ I
6) to be found only in some pieces of KaṭhB, not in KS, cf. present author, KaṭhĀ, annot. 27; on KS, TB, cf. also KEITH, transl. of TS, Harvard Or. Ser., vol. VI p. XCVII.

7) for some peculiarities of KU, having Prākṛtic origin, see ALSDORF, ZDMG, vol. 100, p. 625, 636.
8) for these ritual handbooks, which contain not only *Paddhatis* but also fragments of KS, KaṭhB, KaṭhŚU, KaṭhŚS, KGS, KaṭhDhS etc., see present author, ed. of KaṭhĀ, introduction, annot. 6, and in detail, "The Veda in Kashmir" chapter II (with literature), to be published as Vol. 2 of the monography series of StII, Reinbek 1977 (abbr. VIK)
9) Printed, since 40 years, in the edition of the Laugākṣi-Gṛhyasūtra (LGS/KGS), vol. II p. 92 sqq. — Kashmir Series of Texts and Studies, No. LV, Bombay 1934.

memorising the Veda. This *vrata* contains special rules for learning and teaching the Upaniṣad of the Kaṭha Śākhā, and closely follows the preceding observance, i.e. the *śukriya,*[10] which has to be undertaken when studying the Āraṇyaka (*pravargya mantras* and *brāhmaṇas*). In the exposition of the last mentioned *vrata,* the text of two *śāntis*[11] and also of the first *anuvāka*[12] of the Āraṇyaka is taught. Therefore, one would expect to find in the *aupaniṣada-vrata* not only the *śānti* of the KU, beginning with *saha nā avatu,* but also the first *vallī* of this text, which starts with *uśan ha vai vājaśravasaḥ.*

But instead of this, the *vrata* contains a *śānti* text beginning with *śan no mitraś śaṁ varuṇaḥ,* which unfortunately has been transmitted in all the mss. without accent marks. It corresponds almost completely to TU I 1, and in fact, both DEVAPĀLA, the commentator of the Kāṭhaka-Gṛhyasūtra (KGS, also called Laugākṣi-Gṛhyasūtra : LGS), and the author of the Paddhati [13] based on this Sūtra, refer to this *śānti* as *prathamo 'nuvākaḥ.* The second *śānti* corresponds to TU I 12, and in the further exposition of the *aupaniṣada-vrata,* again some texts are to the found, which have parallels with those of TU I. The prima-facie conclusion to the drawn from these facts, would be to assume that the Kaṭhas took over a part of the *śīkṣāvallī* of the TU and incorporated it into their canonical texts, as they did not yet have an Upaniṣad of their own at the time of redaction of their canonical texts – the well-known KU being of comparatively late origin. This would not be altogether surprising as BHAWE,[14] for instance, assumes a similar procedure in the case of the fifth book of the Kāṭhakam (KS), which contains the *mantras* of the *aśvamedha;* these mostly are parallel to or identical with those of the Taittirīya-Saṁhitā (TS).

3. A more detailed comparision of TU I with the text portion belonging to the *aupaniṣada-vrata,* however, will show that both texts do only differ from each other in deletion or addition of some words, or in using different words to express the same idea, but also in occasional deviation of thought: thus exemplifying the typical relationship of two parallel Vedic texts, belonging to nearly related recensions of one Veda. This impression will also be strengthened by the fact that the above texts, contained in the LGS/KGS and its commentaries, appear with a *sandhi* form typical for the Kaṭha-Śākhā and quite unusual for the Taittirīya-Śākhā.[15]

10) *aupaniṣadaṃ pravargyena vyākhyātam* (*Paddhati* on LGS/KGS). See: *The Veda in Kashmir*, ch. V: The Veda-Vratas of the Kaṭha School
11) ed. KaṭhĀ p. 8 sqq. 11 sqq.
12) ed. KaṭhĀ p. 1–3
13) apparently, ĀDITYADARŚANA, for him and DEVAPĀLA, see CALAND, ed. of KGS, Lahore 1925, introduction.
14) see BHAWE, Die Yajus des Aśvamedha, Stuttgart 1939, p. 55, 58, 70
15) e. g. *nā avatu* K, as opposed to *nāv avatu* T, *asmin sahasra°* K: *tasmint sahasra°* T, *svàr* K ; *súvar* T, etc.. The peculiarities of the older Kashmirian

All of this would point to a separate Kaṭha version of TU I (Śīkṣāvallī). The frequent deviations of the Kaṭha text from TU I, and the peculiarities of *sandhi* etc. identical with those of other Kaṭha texts, do not indicate a simple taking over of TU I into the canonical text corpus of the Kaṭhas but would rather date back to a tradition common to both schools, inherited from the late Brāhmaṇa period.[16]

4. The tradition of the Kaṭha School, however, has been badly affected by Muslim rule in late medieval times even in this *śākhā*'s retreat,[17] i.e. Kashmir, and therefore, only a few fragments [18] of the voluminious canonical texts of the school have survived. Among them, there is no complete manuscript of the Upaniṣad postulated above (3.), and because of this, every statement in literature quoting this text has to be welcomed. In this regard, first of all, the introductory remarks to the *aupaniṣada-vrata* itself have to be taken into consideration. They are found in the Cārāyaṇīya- Mantrārṣādhyāya. After the 'heading' *athopaniṣad,* the mss. have got the following sentence : *Brāhmaṇāṇi Sumantoḥ Kaśyapasya ca tadantevāsināñ copaniṣat* [19] "now follow the Brāhmaṇas (composed) by Sumantu (and) Kaśyapa and the Upaniṣad (composed) by his pupils."[20]

Veda mss. (i.e. homorganic nasal before occlusive, preserving of the Upadhmānīya, etc.) have to be evaluated differently: These are traditional spellings, sometimes also to be found in other areas of India, and also in Nepal (see also StII, Heft 1, p. 107, ann. 103, 104).

16) an agreement, dating back to approximately the same period, is also found in the mantras of the *pravargya* ritual of both schools, in the *mantra* collection used for the *aśvamedha* rite.

17) See: VIK, ch. II

18) See KaṭhĀ, introduction, and below, 10.3

19) VIŚVA BANDHU'S edition, however, reads: *brāhmaṇāni....ca / upaniṣad brahmaṇaḥ*
The Ms. used by him, however, (D.A.V. College, Lahore, now deposited in the VVBVRI, Hoshiarpur, No. 6871) does *not* show this division of the sentences, just like the Ms. Berlin (Staatsbibliothek Preussischer Kulturbesitz, the former Royal Liberary, Ms. Chambers No. 40 = WEBER's Cat. No.) and as well as the Ms. Poona, too (BÜHLER's collection of 1875/76, now deposited in BORI : No. 3: 1875/6), only the modern print of the Upanayana - vidhi (ed. NĀTHA RĀMA ŚĀSTRĪ, Śrīnagar, V. S. 1993, p. 130) abbreviates as follows: *brāhmaṇāni ... cārṣam.* The division of the sentences thus has been made by VIŚVA BANDHU himself.

20) it could also be understood as *Sumantoḥ *Kāśyapasya* 'of Sumantu, the descendent of Kaśyapa', this however has no support in the mss. – Kaśyapa is very famous in Kashmir (see : Rājataraṅgiṇī, etc)., and he is also frequently mentioned in the Cār.M.Ā. (see the edition, index). The alleged composition of the Upaniṣad by Kaśyapa's pupils fits well with its comparative late date, (at least for the famous KU: *uśan ha vai*).Apparently, there seems to exist a relationship between teacher and pupils of the Kaṭha school as it is known from the one of Bodhāyana or Vādhūla and their pupils who composed many texts in their teachers' names.

Unfortunately, the Cār.M.Ā. does not contain *pratīkas* in its last portion, yet this quotation shows that, at least at the time of copying the mss.[21] of the *aupaniṣada-vrata* (the oldest[22] one probably of ca.1500 A.D.), viz. during the time of the author (ĀDITYADARŚAṆA,[23] apparently) of the Paddhati containing this quotation, the said text portions were regarded as belonging to an Upaniṣad of the Kaṭha School.

The commentators of the KGS/LGS, however, even furnish us with more detailed evidence. The author of the paddhati, for instance, here[24] speaks about teaching the 1st, 12th, 13th, 14th Anuvākas, and of a *yajuṣ-śānti*. DEVAPĀLA, too, who still had a much fuller knowledge of the text corpus of the Kaṭha Śākhā than the one to be gained on the basis of existing mss. today, mentions[25] the 1st, 11th and 12th anuvākas. He then specifies this enumeration as the portions [26] beginning with *śan no mitraś, śaṁ varuṇas, śan no bhavaty aryamā,* viz. *satyaṁ vada....*, viz. *śan no mitraś śaṁ varuṇaś śan no astu aryamā,* all of which he quotes in full extent. The parallelism of TU I with its Kaṭha parallel thus even covers the arrangement of single *anuvākas.*

5. The testimony of ŚAṄKARA, however, put this still further back into the past i.e. to the end of the 7th or the beginning of the 8th century. In his commentary on the Brahmasūtra (III 3, 25), he quotes the beginnings of some Upaniṣads:

Asty Ātharvaṇikānām upaniṣadārambhe mantrasāmānayaḥ: "sarvaṃ pravidhya hṛdayaṃ pravidhya dhamanīḥ pravṛjya śiro' bhipravṛjya tridhā vipṛktaḥ" ity ādiḥ / Tāṇḍinām: "deva savitaḥ prasuva yajñam" ity ādiḥ / Śātyāyaninām: "śvetāśvo haritanīlo 'si" ity ādiḥ / Kaṭhānāṃ Taittirīyāṇāṃ ca: "śaṃ no mitraḥ śaṃ varuṇaḥ" ity ādiḥ / Vājasaneyināṃ tūpaniṣadārambhe pravargyabrāhmaṇaṃ pāṭhyate: "deva ha vai sattraṃ niṣeduḥ" ity ādiḥ / Kauṣītakinām apy agniṣṭomabrāhmaṇam: "brahma vā agniṣṭomo brahmaiva tad ahar brahmaṇaiva te brahmopayanti te 'mṛta tvam āpnuvanti ya etad ahar upayanti." iti/

21) RENOU (Éc. véd. p. 151) thinks the Cār.M.Ā. to be a childish effort, expressing the wish to imitate the Ṛgveda Anukramaṇīs – and thus, he apparently regards it as late.

22) Tübingen, University Library, MaI 396 No. 8, see : SCHROEDER, Die Tüb. Kaṭha Hss., p. 29 sqq.

23) he flourished before DEVAPĀLA, (see CALAND, ed, KGS p. VIII), but the antiquity of both of them cannot be ascertained securely enough, see : The Veda in Kashmir, ch. III, 1.

24) See VIK, ch. V, 6

25) LGS II p. 92

26) cf. part II of this article, 11.6 (to be published in the next vol. of the Indo-Iranian Journal)

This comparatively early testimony, which is independent of the school tradition of the Kaṭhas of Kashmir, should suffice to indicate for the Kaṭha śākhā the authenticity of the Upaniṣad texts mentioned above (2,4).[27]

6.1. On the other hand, ŚAṄKARA surprisingly here does not mention the beginning of the much more famous Kaṭhopaniṣad (*uśan ha vai vājaśravasaḥ*) which was well–known to him.[28] A more detailed scrutiny of the text passage quoted above will show that this apparent incongruency is not a mistake in the text of ŚAṄKARA's Bhāṣya:

ŚAṄKARA here counters the objection contending the above-mentioned texts (5) should not be connected with the *vidyas,* (i.e. the knowledge of *ātman, bráhman* etc.,) because they are (only) found in the neighbourhood of Upaniṣad books, in concluding – after a lengthy discussion – this should not be feared only because of the neighbourhood of both kinds of texts, for the proximity of both kinds of texts in the arrangement of the Vedic canons is caused by both being recited in the wilderness (*araṇya*).[29] – This will show clearly that ŚAṄKARA in fact, does not count the texts quoted by him (above § 5) among the Upaniṣads proper. These texts, however, must have been traditionally found near to the Upaniṣads, in the arrangement of the Veda texts of the various schools quoted by him.

6.2. This, in fact, can be proved by scrutinizing the quoted passages: The mantra *deva savitaḥ prasuva yajñam,* attributed to the Tāṇḍins, is to be found in Mantra-Brāhmaṇa I 1, 1 (also called Chāndogya-Br., Mantraparvan, Upaniṣadbrāhmaṇa), i. e. at the beginning of that work of the Kauthuma/ Rāṇāyaṇīya Sāmavedins which also contains their Upaniṣad: ChB I and II= Mantrapāṭha,[30] ChB III–X = ChU.[31]

27) This does not exclude an early inclusion of the texts by the Taitt. school

28) e. g. 1.4.1, where the KU is quoted four times, once with the specification *Kāṭhake* (= KU 1,3, 3–4, 10–13) cf. also ŚAṄKARA'S commentary on KU itself.

29) *upaṇiṣadgranthānāṃ samīpe pāṭhāt:* see also DEUSSEN's translation, p. 587.

30) This is a *mantra* collection made for the Gṛhyasūtra

31) s. BHATTACHARYA, ed. of ChB, Calcutta 1957, p. XX sq.; exactly this order of texts which is found only with the Kauth. and Rāṇ.; the Jaim. put their Up. immediately after their Br., and not only after their GS–Mantrap., see also PARPOLA, The literature and study of the Jaiminīya Sāmaveda, Stud. Orient. XLIII : 6, Helsinki 1973, p. 27. It is important for the history of Veda tradition that this order of texts apparently had been fixed already in ŚAṄKARA's time.

Similarly, the Śāṭyāyanī *mantra: śvetāśvo haritanīlo 'si* is found in a passage neighbouring the Upaniṣad. In this case, however, the situation is somewhat more complicated: As it is well-known, the texts of the Śāṭyāyana and the Jaiminīya schools of the Sāmaveda agree almost word by word with each other.[32] Therefore, one may more or less identify the Jaiminīya-Upaniṣad-brāhmaṇa (JUB) with the lost ŚāṭyUB. The mantra quoted by ŚAṄKARA, however, is to be found in JUB IV 1. 1 as *śvetāśvo darśato harinīlo 'si* i.e. in a form slightly different[33] from the one quoted above. This passage occurs shortly before the Kena-Upaniṣad (= JUB IV 18 – 21) and thus also at the begining of a *brāhmaṇa* text which includes the Upaniṣad. Yet ŚAṄKARA probably might have meant something else, for JUB IV 17, 2 says:

saiṣā śāṭyāyanī gāyatrasyopaniṣad evam upāsitavyā

'as such, this Gāyatrī–Upaniṣad of Śāṭyāyanī has thus to be revered.'

This sentence refers to the passages JUB IV 11–16 preceding the passage immediately; and it is followed in IV 17, 1 by a list of teachers also containing the name of Śāṭyāyanī.

Therefore, the text portion now included into JUB IV 11–17 could well have formed the *upaniṣad* of the Śāṭyāyanīs.[34] If this is correct, ŚAṄKARA's quotation would also be found in the immediate neighbourhood of the *upaniṣad* of the Śāṭyāyanīs.[35]

The next passage quoted by ŚAṄKARA, however, creates a slightly different problem: The mantra *śaṃ no mitraḥ śam no varunaḥ* is said to be found next to the *Upaniṣad* of the Taittirīyas. Yet, in this school, the *mantra* is traced only in TU I 1 (and 12) i.e. at the beginning (viz. at the end) of the first

32) See, e.g., the many quotations from ŚāṭyB brought together by GHOSH, Lost Brāhmaṇas, Calcutta 1947, and their close parallels in JB; cf. also OERTEL, JAOS 18 (1897) p. 15 sqq. and, slightly differently, PARPOLA, The Lit. and Study, p. 7, 9, 27 (ŚāṭyB = oldername of JB)

33) Without v. l. in OERTEL, ed. JUB p. 201; both parallel versions here exhibit the typical slight disagreement of two recensions of the same school text.

34) Similarly, already, OERTEL, JAOS 18, p. 25, he nevertheless thinks *śvetāśvo haritanīlo 'si* to be the beginning of the Up., and not of the Brāhmaṇa preceding the Up. – His reference to still another, different ŚāṭyUp. (India Office Library, Cat. Ved. Mss., No. 3183, part 118), however, is worth mentioning.

35) Supposing the two recensions here are so close to each other as characterised above. – Perhaps, one may assume that the Up. Br. of the Śāṭy. already ended with the passage corresponding to JUB IV 17, and JUB IV 18–28 (including the Kena-Up.) are an addition of the Jaim.

part of the text traditionally[36] called Taittirīya-Upaniṣad itself. This would be contrary to the relationship existing between the passages quoted above (5.) and the *upaniṣads* of their respective *śākhās* (cf., however, below 7.)

The two following quotations, however, are clear again: The Pravargya-brāhmaṇa of the Vājasaneyins (i.e. their Āraṇyaka, Bṛhadāraṇyaka) infact starts with the words: *deva ha vai sattraṃ niṣeduḥ* (= Śatapatha-Brāhmaṇa, Mādhyandina recension XIV 1. 1. 1 = Kāṇva recension XVI 1. 1. 1.). The exposition of the *pravargya* is immediately followed in both schools of the Vājasaneyi *śākhā* by the Upaniṣad (ŚBM XIV 4, 1, 1 = ŚBK XVII 3.3.1)[37]. A similar relationship can be found of the quotation from the *agniṣṭoma brāhmaṇa* of the Kauṣītakins: *brahma* vā *agniṣṭomo... upayanti* is traced in Kauṣītaki-Āraṇyaka (KĀ II 18, at the end) and therefore immediately before the Upaniṣad which begins with KĀ III.

The result of an investigation of the mantras and prose passages quoted by Śaṅkara and their relationship with the Upaniṣads, as far as these are transmitted until today, (for TU cf. below §7) thus everywhere is the same:

The quotations are to be found in texts which have been handed down in immediate neighbourhood to the Upaniṣads of the respective Vedic schools. Only the quotation *sarvaṃ pravidhya,* attributed to the Ātharvins cannot be traced.[38] The reason for this has to be sought in the fact that the said *mantra* stems from an unknown, not yet discovered Brāhmaṇa, apparently

36) The various parts, however, frequently are named seperately: TĀ VII—Śīkṣāvallī, VIII — Ānandavallī, IX — Bhṛguvallī; VIII and IX are grouped together as Vāruṇī-Up. by the Ātreyī-Śākhā, see Deussen, 60 Up., p. 213 sq.

37) The Kāṇvas, however, have put a short passage corresponding to ŚB (M) X 6, 4–5 before their Up. As the BĀU mostly is read in the recension of the Kāṇvas, because it had been commented on by Śaṅkara, BĀU (K) I 1.1 is equal to ŚBK XVI 1. 1 = ŚBM X 6. 4; only beginning with BĀU (K) 1.3, both versions run parallel to each other.

38) *not* to be found in: Vedic Word Conocordande by Vishva Bandhu, i.e. not contained in AV (Śaun.), GB etc, also not to be found in the Kashmir Ms. of AV (Paipp.) : in any case, the looked for passage is from an AV–Āraṇyaka or from the portion of the AV–Br., preceding the Up. immediately.

the Paippalāda-Br.[39] This must either have contained Āraṇyaka-like[40] materials, or it must immediately have preceded the "Atharvaveda-Upaniṣad" meant by ŚAṄKARA. In his time this Brāhmaṇa, which consisted of 8 *adhyāyas*, apparently still was known well.[41]

Now, the only exception from the rule governing the relationship of ŚAṄKARA's quotations and the respective Upaniṣads is the quotation adduced for the Kaṭhas and Taittirīyas: It is found at the beginning (viz. also at the end) of the first section of the Upaniṣad itself.

7. However, when applying the results of the investigation of the other quotations to the *mantra* quoted for the Kaṭhas and Taittirīyas, too, one can only conclude that ŚAṄKARA thought the Śīkṣāvallī of the Taittirīyas (TU I = TĀ VII) to have been handed down only in *connection* with the Upaniṣad of the Taittirīyas, but did not regard it as being of Upaniṣad type.[42]

This conclusion is to some extent confirmed by the order of the texts of the Taittirīyas in the Anukramaṇī of the Ātreyī *śākhā*: here, text portions belonging to the Saṁhitā (TS) and the Brāhmaṇa (TB I–III 9 with insertion of TĀ III–IV), are followed by the Śīksāvallī (TĀ VII), and the Nārāyaṇa-

39) according to the Prapañcahṛdaya (TSS No. XLV p. 21) an extensive texr of 8 *adhyāyas : tathātharvaṇike paippalādaśākhāyām mantro viṁśatikāṇḍaḥ/ . . ./ tad brāhmaṇam adhyāyāṣṭakam* / "In the Paippalāda school of the Atharvadeva, the *mantra* (portion, i.e. the Saṁhitā) is 20 *Kāṇḍas*... The Brāhmaṇa of that (school) is of eight *adhyāyas*....–" It should supprise that the *mantra* in question is not to be found in the GB:. This is a relatirely late work (partly, even post-Pāṇineian : Karl HOFFMANN once pointed out to me that GB I 16 has a set of Pāṇineian phraseology = Prāṇava–Up., see DEUSSEN, 60 Up., p. 859 sqq.), which presupposes most of the other Brāhmaṇas quoted by it explicity. It easily could have included the portion meant by ŚAṄKARA, and still could have preceded the Up. of the Ātharvins (it is not clear which one is meant by ŚAṄKARA here) i.e. in the traditional order of texts of this school. – If, however, the GB was only an *anubrāhmaṇa*, (perhaps appended to Paipp. B.), the non-occurence of the *mantra* in GB should not surprise, cf. e.g. VādhB (see StII, 1 p. 81 sqq.) versus TS–TB–TĀ–TU : the GB now known to us cold be younger than the Up. meant by ŚAṄKARA.

40) ŚAṄKARA *: evam anyeṣām api mantrāṇām... rahasyapaṭhitānām* "likewise, of the other mantras (i.e. not the *mantras* quoted as *sarvam pravidhya*, and : *deva savituḥ*), recited in the *rahasya* (text = Āraṇyaka)"

41) The mantra quoted by him thus was known to him also in its application: *abhicārikaviṣayo hy eso 'rthaḥ* "Its meaning is : it belongs to the subject of sorcery" (which, however, could also be understood easily from the very words of the *mantra*).

42) Whether he meant TU I 1 or I 12, when quoting *saṃ no mitraḥ*

upaniṣad (TĀ X), and only then by the real Taittirīya-Upaniṣad,[43] i.e. TĀ VIII (Ānandavallī) and TĀ IX (Bhṛguvallī).[44] Both ŚAṄKARA's opinion and the order of the Ātreyī- *śākhā* are further substantiated, when looking at the contents of the Śīksāvallī: Very little, indeed, is to be found there that usually is regarded as Upaniṣad-like material, and this is to be found in quite unorderly sequence and mixed with texts not to be regarded as Upaniṣads. The Upaniṣad-like portions (TU I 2.3.5–10), too, have more or less to be regarded as beginning but not as developed upaniṣadic speculation: one can for example find the early series of identifications of microcosm and macrocosm. As for the rest of the Śīkṣāvallī, i.e. the sections indicated above (§§ 1, 4), concerning the study of the Veda and its secret meaning, such materials are often not contained in the Upaniṣads of others *śākhās* but these too, belong to the Āraṇyaka.[45]

8. Of special importance, however, for the knowledge of the corpus of canonical texts of the Kaṭha school, is the early evidence furnished by ŚAṄKARA's quotation, and the inherent classification of the *anuvākas* beginning with *śaṃ no mitraḥ śam no varuṇaḥ* as a text transmitted next to the Upaniṣad of this school.

On one hand, it shows that these *anuvākas* belonged to a longer version of the Kaṭha-Upaniṣad just as the Kauṣītaki–Up. is a part of the Kauṣītaki-Āraṇyaka[46] or the Kena–Up. a portion of the Jaiminīya-Upaniṣad–Brāhmaṇa. On the other hand, ŚAṄKARA's classification of the *anuvākas* constituting the Kaṭha–Śīkṣā-Upaniṣad, indicates that the longer Kaṭha-Up. also contained some material, not known to us now-a-days. Partly, this will have been a parallel version of TU I 2–3, 5–10, i.e. of those portions not taught in connection with the rules for the *aupaniṣada-vrata* which, nevertheless, must have belonged to the Kaṭh ŚU as is to be inferred from the *anuvāka* numeration. Yet as these *anuvākas* did, according to ŚAṄKARA, not belong to the Upaniṣad proper, it remains to be answered, actualy *what* he regarded as such.

43) i. e. the Vāruṇī-Up. (see above)

44) The list is concluded by the *aṣṭau kāṭhakāni,* taken over from the Kaṭhas.

45) See, e.g., Ait. Ār. 3, Kauṣ. Ār. 7–8

46) This would mean : KaṭhĀ – KaṭhU – KaṭhĀ. This would be supported by CALAND's inclusion of many small texts not belonging to the *pravargya* rite, into KaṭhĀ (see, KGS passim, and : Versl. Kg. Akad. Amsterdam 1920 p. 467 sqq.); cf., also : edition of the KaṭhĀ, introduction, annot. 37, and VIK, ch. V and VIII (Veda Vratas, Text Corpus of the Kaṭha School).

9. As both the Kaṭha and the Taittirīya *śākhā* exhibit a far reaching parallelism in many of their younger texts, [47] one could be led to assume that this would also hold true for the Upaniṣad of both schools, and therefore, a parallel version of TĀ VIII – IX or X would have belonged to the canonical texts of the Kaṭhas, as this clearly is the the case with TĀ VII (with some variants, of course). In this case, the famous Kaṭhopaniṣad (*uśan ha vai...*) would in the old canon of this school have followed only after these texts.

Some parts of TĀ X, the Nārāyaṇa-Up., actually can be traced in the texts contained in the *aupaniṣada-vrata,* and even elsewhere, but a parallel version of TĀ VIII – IX, (of the main Taittirīya–Up.), cannot be found anywhere in the Ṛcakas, if I have seen correctly. This is substantiated by the medieval commentators, (s. § 4) who still were much better informed on this *śākhā* than we are now: DEVAPĀLA[48] still knows 15 *anuvākas* which were regarded as Upaniṣad:

tatra śatādhyayana upaniṣattvena prasiddheṣv anuvākeṣu pañcadaśasu prathamaikādaśadvādaśānām ihopayogo' sti

"Here (in the *aupaniṣada vrata*), use is made of the 1st, the 11th, and the 12th in the Śatādhyaya of the 15 *anuvākas,* known of having Upaniṣad character, (= KaṭhB)." Just like ŚAṄKARA's statement (s. § 8), this passage from DEVAPĀLA also indicates that the Kaṭh ŚU was part of a longer text, which here is called Śatādhyaya(na). [49] This is the name frequently employed in the Ṛcakas to designate the fragments of the Kaṭha-Brāhmaṇa. Because of DEVAPĀLA's statement, it can safely be deducted that this lost Brāhmaṇa also included the Āraṇyaka and the Upaniṣad.

The author[50] of the Paddhati of the *aupaniṣada-vrata* is even more clear about the extent of the text:

47) See above, annot 14, on the *Aśvamedha,* and on the *pravargya* mantras, cf. also the inclusion of texts into TB III 10–TĀ II and certain paralles between Kaṭha fragments and TĀ X.

48) LGS, Vol. II, p. 92

49) for this designation, see also CALAND, Aanwinsten p. 467, 483, ann. 1., SŪRYAKĀNTA, Kāṭhaka-saṃkalanam, Lahore 1943, p. 4 ann. 10 (the *śatādhyaya* quotations from JAYANTA BHAṬṬA are to be found on p. 236 of the Chowkhamba ed. of the Nyāyamanjarī; for JAYANTA's knowledge of the Vedas, see VIK, ch. IV) cf. also SCHROEDER, SB Wien 1896 p. 12 (= name of KS XL 11 etc).

50) viz. of the Sūtra, from which these sentences apparently have been taken see : VIK , ch. V; here reproduced according to the following Mss. : Paris, National Library (Bibliothèque Nationale), ms. dév. 230 fol. 316a (=P), dated (17)80 A.D.; Paris, ms. dév. 227b, fol 16a (= P_2); Tübingen University Library (Universitätsbibliothek), Ma I 396, fol. 286b (= t_1)

nainam eko[51] *'dhīyīthaḥ*[52] /[52] *mā*[53] *bahavo 'dhīyadhvam:*[54] *dvāv*[55] *evādhīyīthāḥ:*[56] *prathamadvādaśau śāntir dvādaśānāṃ trayodaśaścaturdaśayoḥ*[57] *prathamaṃ yajuśśāntiḥ* / [58] *evam*[59] ante[59]

"You shall not study this text being alone (just one person), you shall not study (it, being) many (a group); you must study it, (being) two (teacher and pupil only, i.e. secretly) : the first and the twelvth (*anuvāka*) of the (group of) twelve (= KaṭhŚU) as (general) *śānti*, and the first (anuvāka) of (the group forming) the 13th and the 14th (anuvāka) as the *Yajuḥ-Śānti;* at the end (of the *vrata*) in the same way."[60]

10.1. As the KaṭhŚU 1–12 is parallel to TU I, it is quite open what could be meant by 13th, 14th, and 15th *anuvākas* (see 8). If an evaluation of the text portion quoted in the *aupaniṣada-vrata* is based on a comparison with those of the *śukriya-vrata,* which forms its *prakṛti,*[61] *anuvākas* 1 and 12 of the KaṭhŚU correspond to the *pūrvā* and *uttarā śānti* of the *śukriya-vrata.* This actually is taught by the commentators. If one then excludes the *mantras* contained in *anuvāka* 4, because of their special application, the portion corresponding to the 1st *anuvāka* of the text to be taught during the time of the *śukriya-vrata* would be missing. The teaching of this *anuvāka,* in fact, is expressively ordered by the Paddhati: "the 1st (*anuvāka*) of (the group forming) the 13th and 14th".

In this context, it should be noticed that the famous Kaṭhopanisad usually is divided into 6 *vallīs,* but also is found divided into TWO *adhyāyas,* which differ considerably from each other in their contents. It cannot be excluded that these two short text portions, comprising only 71 viz. 48 verses, formed the two *anuvākas* (14 and 15)[62] left unaccounted for by DEVAPĀLA.

51) *eka* pr. manu, *eko* sec. manu P_2
52) *daṇḍa* is missing in t_1; *dhīyethāḥ* P
53) for the rare occurrence of *mā* with Optative in late Vedic, especially when already preceded by an Optative, cf. K. HOFFMANN, Injunktiv, p. 97.
54) *dhīyadha* [ ] : pasted over, t_1, *dhīyīdhvam* P
55) pasted over t_1
56) *eva* in t_1 written with e– ए; *dvāvīvo* pr. manu (?), *dvāveva* sec. manu P, *visarga* in °*thāḥ* sec. manu P, °*yethāḥ* P_2
57) *trayo*[ ]*catur* t_1 (pasted over)
58) °*tiḥ* (visarga !) t_1, °*tiḥ* P_2, *yajuḥśāntir* P
59) *evam* ante t_1 (with e–), *evam* (with e–) *evānte* P_2, *eva/mante* P
60) the meaning "many (*anuvākas*) (should be studied)" is excluded by nom. pl. *bahavaḥ*.
61) see above annot.
62) The parallel structure of *śukriyavrata* (Āraṇyaka) and *aupaniṣadavrata* (Upaniṣad) would then also imply the teaching of the first section (of the Āraṇyaka, of the Upaniṣad); see VIK, ch. V: Veda-Vratas

In this case, the question of the identity of the 'Yajuḥ-Śānti' remains to be answered. It could have been the short, non-metrical formula (*saha nā avatu*),[63] attached to the 1st and 12th anuvāka, in the *aupanisada-vrata*. This cannot, however, be stated with certainity as long as further materials could not be found, or a manuscript of the longer Upaniṣad would turn up somewhere.

These 15 *anuvākas* constituted the *Upaniṣat-saṁhitā* of the Kaṭhas (as DEVAPĀLA once calls it), i.e. the Kaṭha-Upaniṣad in its *larger* sense, The complex character of *this* Upaniṣad is also indicated by DEVAPĀLA's expression (i.e. Saṁhitā): The well-known Kaṭhopaniṣad (beginning with *uśan ha vai vājaśravasaḥ*) apparently formed only *anuvākas* 14 and 15 of the *larger* Kaṭha-Upaniṣad.

10.2. This will also explain[64] that besides the traditional names Kaṭhopaniṣad or Kāṭhakopaniṣad,[65] the designation 'Kaṭhavallyupaniṣad' also occurs: The shorter Kaṭhavallyupaniṣad had to be distinguished from the larger (Kaṭha) Upaniṣad (here called KaṭhŚU), of which it only formed a part, just as the Kena-Up. had to be distinguished from the surrounding Jaiminīya-Upaniṣadbrāhmaṇa.

When this Upaniṣad and the Kaṭhopaniṣad and been taken out from their surrounding texts, and an independent line of tradition had begun with the collection of all Upaniṣads, in connection with the Vedānta system, which was since then independent from Vedic tradition, – the old connection, still known to ŚAṄKARA, of the Śikṣā - Up. with the Kaṭha school

63) Thus, this *śānti* (*saha nā avatu*) would immediately have preceded the KU (*uśan ha vai*) and would in this way have become its *śānti,* as it secundarily also has become the *śānti* of TĀ VII (and VIII). – However, one could also think of the small text portion parallel to TĀ X 7 (*dhāraṇam me 'stu*), which clearly refers to the wish not to forget the text once it has been learned : This could have formed the 15th *anuvāka,* especially if the passage refered to above could be read as:

trayodaśacaturdaśayoḥ prathamaṃ. yajuśśāntir evam ante.
"(you shall learn) the first (*anuvāka*) of the (group forming the) 13th and 14th. The *yajuḥ śānti* likewise, at the end."

64) i.e. if the KU was included into the larger Kaṭha-Up., or, better: attached to it because KaṭhŚU 11 already forms the *conclusion* of Veda study and the transition to the life of a householder.

65) See New Catalogus Catalogorum, s. v. The Ka(ṇ)ṭha-śruty-upaniṣad (Cat. India Office Library, No. 494, pt. 101 = Ms. No 3188) is a late Vedic text, ending in *ślokas,* and which has nothing to do with the theme of KU. The text of the India Office ms. is remarkably longer at the end than the text translated by DEUSSEN (60 Up., p. 700 sqq.)

could be forgotten. This was facilitated by the fact that the Kaṭha *śākhā* has been preserved only in Kashmir, while the Upaniṣad collection mainly had been transmitted in South India.[66]

Though originally all the 15 anuvākas mentioned by DEVAPĀLA probably were called Kaṭhopaniṣad or perhaps also (Kaṭha-) Upaniṣat-saṁhitā, it will be more practical to retain by now traditional designation "Kaṭhopaniṣad" for the verse dialogue of Naciketas and Yama (beginning with *uśan ha vai...*), and to introduce the name Kaṭha-Śikṣā-Upaniṣad (KaṭhŚU) for the Kaṭha texts corresponding to TU I. This also is warranted by the colophons of the extant mss.[67]

10.3. The order of the texts that had constituted the canon of the Kaṭha *Śākhā* and their relations with the Taittirīya *śākhā* can now be depicted as follows:

Śatādhyaya-Brāhmaṇa

KAṬHA-SAṀHITĀ (Kāṭhakam) in 5 *granthas* (viz. 40 *sthānakas*+13 *Aśva-medha-anuvacanas*)	~	TAITTIRĪYA-SAṀHITĀ (*Aśvamedha-Mantras* in TS)
KAṬHA-BRĀHMAṆA (Preserved only in fragments, e. g.		TAITTIRĪYA-BRĀHMAṆA
–*Caturhotṛ mantras*	~	(–*Caturhotṛmantras*—) TĀ III 1–6)
–*special Agnicayanas*	⟶	TB III 10–12, TĀ I
–*Svādhyāya-br.*, etc.	⟶	TĀ II
KAṬHA-ĀRAṆYAKA (*Pravargaya- Mantras* and –*Brāhmaṇa*)	~	TAITTIRĪYA-ĀRAṆYAKA TĀ IV TĀ V
KAṬHA-UPANIṢAT–(SAṀHITĀ) *Śikṣā-Up.*: 1,4,11,12 (etc.) *Yajuśśānti* (13th *anuvāka*) *Kaṭhopaniṣad:* 14, 15 (— *uśan ha vai......*)	~	TAITTIRĪYA-UPANIṢAD TU I = TĀ VII, partly TĀ X

66) See Deussen, Sechzig Upanishad's des Veda

67) Thus, e. g., Paris dév. 230, Tübingen MaI 396, fol. 266a, Paris dév. 227b, 14b : *iti śikṣā,* after KaṭhŚU 11 (which is to be found in a reversed position, after KGS 3); also in analogy to the name of TU I : *Śikṣāvallī.*

68) This order exactly fits the one of the *vedavratas* of the Kaṭha School (see: VIK, ch. V) :

1. *Traividyaka – vrata* (KS, KaṭhB)
2. *Cāturhotṛka – vrata* (for the *caturhotṛ* formulae, which are partly to be found in KS IX 8, 9 : *cittis sruk,–* and which,

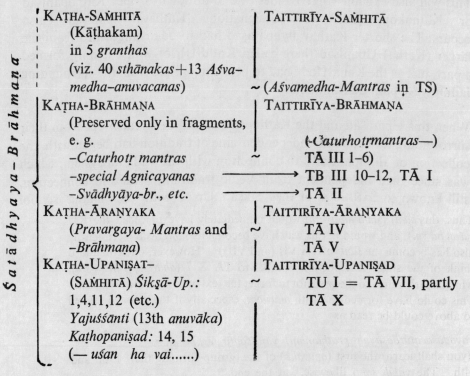

also in the Maitr. school, are learnt seperately, see MGS; in the Kaṭha School they apparently are part of KaṭhB~TĀ III 1–6

3. *Śukriya-vrata* — to learn the *pravargya mantras* and *brāhmaṇas*, i.e. the KaṭhĀ
4. *Āruṇa-vrata* — to learn special way of piling the *agnicayana* : (*aruṇa-ketuka*) → TĀ I
5. *Aupaniṣada-vrata* — to learn the Upaniṣad of the Kaṭhas
6. *Traividyaka-vrata – apavarga* : concluding the Traividya observance; appropriately placed at the very end of the Veda Study, which is concluded by bath and *madhuparka* (today, KaṭhŚU 11 is placed at this point and not earlier)

(The placing of the *Śukriya-vrata* before the *Āruṇa-vrata* may have been caused by the *Śukriya-vrata* forming the *prakṛiti* for all *vratas* dealing with secret doctrines *(rahasya, upaniṣad)*.

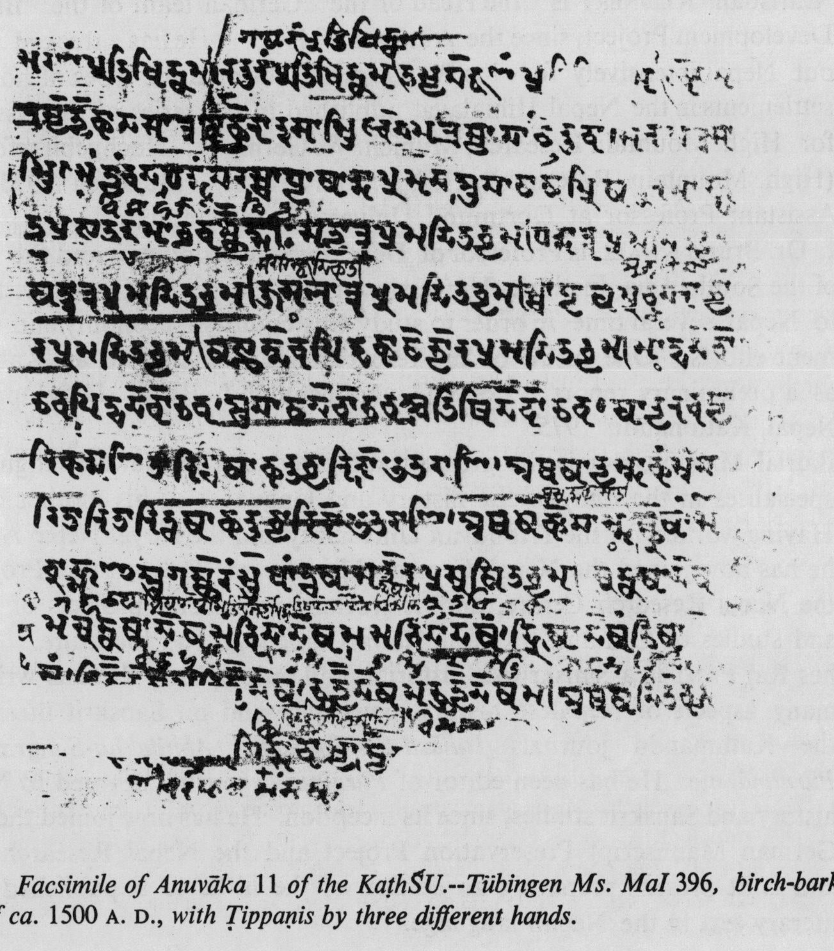

Facsimile of Anuvāka 11 *of the KaṭhŚU.--Tübingen Ms. MaI* 396, *birch-bark, of ca.* 1500 A. D., *with Ṭippaṇis by three different hands.*

Contributors to this Volume

Manabajra BAJRACHARYA is a well-known Ayurvedic physician and scholar. He has written some books on Nepalese art and culture.

Dr. Niels GUTSCHOW, Technical University, Darmstadt, W. Germany, first came to Nepal for the Pūjārī Maṭh Restoration Project. Again, he stayed at Bhaktapur several times (1974–76) to carry out research on the town's religion, history, and sociology. This is part of a project, together with Dr. Bernhard Kölver, sponsored by the Deutsche Forschungsgemeinschaft (German Research Society). A preliminary report of this research has been published as Vol. 1 of the present series.

Dr. Karel Rijk van KOOIJ is Professor of South Asian Art and Archaeology at the University of Utrecht, The Netherlands. He came to Nepal several times to persue his studies of Nepalese Art and to get microfilms from the National Archives for the edition of the *Kubjikāmata-Tantra,* prepared by the Sanskrit Institute of the Utrecht University. He has published an annotated translation of the *Kālikā-Purāṇa* (Leiden, 1972).

Dr. Christian KLEINERT is the Head of the German team of the Bhaktapur Development Project, since the Autumn of 1975. He has trecked throughout Nepal intensively for his Ph. D. dissertation on the types of houses and settlements in the Nepal Himalaya, published in the series of the Association for High Mountain Research, Munich. W. Germany: Hochgebirgsforschung (High Mountain Research), Heft 4, Innsbruck – München 1973. He is Assistant Professor at Dortmund University, W. Germany.

Prof. Dr. Bruno KNALL is Professor of Development Economics and the Director of the South Asia Institute, University of Heidelberg, W. Germany. He came to Nepal several times in order to study this country's economy and development efforts. One result of his research has been printed at Kathmandu as a preliminary report: Local Government and Rural Development in Nepal, Kathmandu 1975.

Thakurlal MANANDHAR is the greatest authority on Old Newari language and specialises in the study of the history and languages of his mother country. Having worked for the Tribhuvan Universtity and the Royal Nepal Academy, he has now joined the Nepal–German Manuscript Preservation Project and the Nepal Research Centre, and is working on several projects of editions and studies of Old and Modern Newari language and literature.

Mahes Raj PANT is a Sanskritist, historian and epigraphist. He has written on many aspects of Nepalese history, epigraphy and on Sanskrit literature in the Kathmandu journals *Itihāsa-Saṁśodhana, Abhilekha-Saṅgraha* and *Pūrṇimā,* etc. He has been editor of *Pūrṇimā,* a journal devoted to Nepalese history and Sanskrit studies, since its inception. He has now joined the Nepal-German Manuscript Preservation Project and the Nepal Research Centre, and is at present preparing an edition of the hitherto unpublished oldest literary text in the Nepali language.

Prof. Dr. Heimo RAU is Professor of South Asian Art at the South Asia Institute, University of Heidelberg, W. Germany, and also the Director of the South Asian Branches of the Goethe Institute (German Cultural Centres, or Max Mueller Bhavans in India). Having visited Nepal frequently since 1960, he has been responsible for the Pūjārī Maṭh Restoration in 1971–72 and for the Goethe Institute, Kathmandu, since its founding in 1975. He has written numerous articles and books on various aspects of Indian and Nepalese art. Beginning with August 1977, he will undertake a detailed study of the Nepalese pagoda style and its wood-carvings, a project sponsored by the Deutsche Forschungsgemeinschaft (German Research Society).

Aishvaya Dhar SHARMA has contributed some papers on Nepalese history and epigraphy in *Itihāsa-Saṁśodhana* and *Saṁskṛta-Sandeśa.* He has now joined the Nepal–German Manuscript Preservation Project.

Dr. Michael WITZEL has been responsible for the Nepal–German Manuscript Preservation project since Sept. 1972, and has been the Representative of the Nepal Research Centre since two years. Besides his official work, he has undertaken a project of collecting microfilms of important Vedic manuscripts in India (1973-74) and a documentation (by filming) of various Vedic rituals in the Kathmandu Valley (1974 sqq.). Both projects have been sponsored by the German Research Society (Deutsche Forschungsgemeinschaft). He has published some articles on Vedic literature and on Nepalese Brahmins and their tradition, and also an edition and English translation of the Kaṭha Āraṇyaka, a pre–Buddhist text dealing with a secret rite and doctrine of the Yajur–veda. (Nepal Research Centre Publications, No. 2.)